NOW FOR THE BACK NINE

Published by Zsazseva Ltd
www.zsazseva.com

ISBN: 978-0-9565771-7-7

British Library Cataloguing-in-Publication Data: A catalogue record for this book is available from the British Library.

Concept, art direction, compilation & edit by Penny Ericson, Simon Hawkins and Jezz Ellwood
Designed by Hilite Design & Reprographics

Photographs by Matt Dunkinson

Printed and bound in Slovakia by Neografia
Stocks from sustainable sources

NOW FOR THE BACK NINE

With best Wishes
Peter

Happy Go Lucky!

Peter Dawson

with

Simon Hawkins

You know you're a back-niner when…

'your mind is trapped in youth and your body has begun to sag, bulge and wrinkle. It's the time when you realise you only need to ask yourself for approval and you're content to power on with a little less speed and a touch more grace.'

'you can actually hear the ball land and on those days of preferred lies you can't face continually bending over to clean and place and think sod it I am sure that big blob of mud won't make that much difference!'

'you need your own personal coaching manual.'

'you go into a blind panic when the ball collector on the end of your putter grip falls off in the middle of a round!'

Thanks Lizzy for the past 40 years.
Now for the Back Nine!

Some wise words from a couple of old back-niner friends

Peter and Tony getting to grips with their putting.

'*When I die, bury me on the golf course so my husband will visit.*

— Unknown'

Tony Jacklin

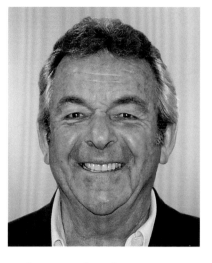

I've known Peter for longer than I care to remember and still recall his early days on tour, especially as he played 'the wrong way around'! Peter is in the history books for being the first left-hander to play in the Ryder Cup but I assure you, there's nothing the wrong way around about his approach to golf for the player of advancing years.

My first recollection of playing with Peter was at Lytham in 1974. It was his first Open. I had won the last time Lytham hosted it in 1969. In '74 I was never in contention but there was still a hullabaloo about me returning to the scene of my victory. The crowds that followed us were large and at times noisy. Despite it being his Open debut, Peter was calm and took it all with such grace. We tied for 18th place miles behind the inspiring champion, Gary Player. It was a wonderful tournament that forged our lasting friendship serendipitously to be furthered when we were back at Lytham in 1977, this time on the same Ryder Cup team.

Golf is so different today from when we graced the fairways at Lytham. Then, the game was about tempo, feel and good imagination. Today it's all about power and putting. Back then hitting a ball 300 yards was a spectacle. Now we'd be considered short-hitters at best!

I enjoy staying current with modern techniques but how on earth can a guy my age be expected to contort himself like that? So it's about time that someone thought kindly of us old boys and came up with some useful advice on how to cope with advancing age and receding shots. *Now for the Back Nine* is for us, written by one of us. Peter reminds us of things we learned long ago and since forgotten. No myths, no quick fixes, just no-nonsense advice that works, from someone who truly understands the golf swing and the game.

Peter has given us a golfing companion. It's a wonderful mix of history, how equipment has evolved, insightful quotes from some of the greats and often hilarious anecdotes from his time on tour.

Tony Jacklin.

Golf and sex are about the only things you can enjoy without being good at.

– Jimmy Demaret

Peter Alliss

Many years ago the great Henry Cotton told me that once you get over 60 years of age you lose 10 yards off your drive every year. I thought what a lot of utter rubbish but, of course, he was right. Golf gets no easier as you get older but there are little ways of improving the skills you have. May I suggest some that may shock you but I am at that stage in my life now where shocking a few people doesn't alarm me anymore, so here goes.

When you're getting to the stage when you feel you're about to give up the game of golf – you know what I mean, no longer can you pick a ball cleanly off the fairway, you can't get out of bunkers etc. etc. and you feel the whole thing is a waste of time, may I make some suggestions. Contrary to all the rules and regulations if, and I repeat if, you're only playing with your own circle of friends and not in any way in a proper competition I hope these few tips will serve you well. If you can no longer hit the ball very far don't be ashamed of going to the most forward tee, once on the fairway use a tee peg, (you'll find that little rescue club will suddenly be hitting ball in the air and you'll be getting on or near a green that you haven't been close to in 2 for 20 years), don't worry if you touch the sand in bunkers, pick up all 2 foot putts.

Follow these simple rules and the smile will return to your faces and you'll keep going and enjoy your golf for many more years. Sorry R & A if that offends you but it's a fact of life. Amongst friends the rules can be bent to nobody's detriment.

Good golfing

Best wishes

CONTENTS

CONTENTS

Peter & Simon

*If you think it's hard to
meet new people,
try picking up the wrong golf ball.*
— Jack Lemmon

Peter

Golf. It's been my game for over 50 years – most of them pretty good and many great. I played for England as an amateur before turning pro in 1970. I played the European Tour for ten years. On reflection I wish that in those early days I had been coached by the Peter Dawson of today, as I know my technical knowledge and experiences on tour would have guaranteed me better results than I achieved.

1977 was my most memorable year. I was selected as a member of the Ryder Cup team, winning my singles against former USPGA Champion, Don January and also partnered Nick Faldo for England in the World Cup.

I've had enormous fun playing all over the world, winning or tying for victory on three occasions and regularly finishing in the top ten before bringing in the new millennium by joining the Senior European Tour in 2000, with some success.

I played with most of the great players of my era including: Tom Watson, Gary Player, Arnold Palmer, Tony Jacklin, Greg Norman, Severiano Ballesteros, Bernhard Langer, Lee Trevino, Ray Floyd, Tom Weiskopf, Bob Charles and Roberto de Vicenzo. In all, I played with the winners of 46 majors, then there were the great players who never won a major such as Peter Alliss, Dave Thomas, Tommy Horton and Neil Coles. The list of greats goes on and on. I've had a wonderful career and enjoyed every minute.

The great thing about golf is that it's not just a sport for the young. I'm still at it – golf that is. I still love it as much as ever although mainly these days as a coach who plays the occasional pro-am.

I've been privileged to coach the International squads of Denmark, Switzerland and Morocco. I'm also proud to be a PGA Master Professional and an Honorary Member of the British PGA.

I've picked up a few things along the way and on the following pages I thought I'd share some of them with you.

If you recognise that patronising look when failing to do what your pro has asked or are beginning to feel a bit like a lost cause because of your physical constraints, read on my friend because this book was written for you.

Why would anyone write a book
about old man's golf?
Better still – why would anyone read it?

*The older you get,
the stronger the wind gets;
and it's always in your face.*
    – Jack Nicklaus

I like chatting with younger golf pros about the mechanics and movement of the modern swing, which is much more physically demanding and only likely to suit a young athletic body. When I explain that some of these movements are difficult, if not impossible, with a stiff back, dicky knees and old war wounds, they tend to look blank as there's little understanding of how to adapt modern teaching to us old'uns.

Nowadays I experience the same problems as other golfers when they reach their 50's or as I like to refer to it, start their back nine. I'm always trying to get back those lost yards and my body increasingly refuses to obey. Were I to sign up for a course of lessons, I'd find myself an experienced pro who understands first-hand the challenges age throws at us.

My credentials and experiences have given me an excellent insight into how the golf swing works for people of different ages, physiques, strengths and weaknesses. Although some of my ideas may seem contradictory to the 'perfect technique', my aim is to find ways that enable us to overcome our increasingly inflexible physiques.

Over the years we've seen many a new fangled idea come and go, some for the better and some for the financial benefit of others, but you can't re-invent the wheel and that's essentially all the golf swing really is!

Players such as Nick Faldo, Tom Watson, Tony Jacklin, Tom Weiskopf, Gary Player, Greg Norman and Severiano Ballesteros played at the highest level for many years because of their common-sense techniques. I've had the pleasure of playing with them and many other great players during my career and this has given me an invaluable knowledge of the game.

Gimmicks work for a day but not long term. There's a saying that for every action there's a reaction. Golf is a game of chain reactions. Start wrong and the whole swing will be wrong. Start with the basics 100% correct and there's a good chance of playing to a very respectable standard.

Introducing exhibit A

In 2016 I was contacted by Simon, a man in his 60's, who was looking for a series of lessons that could specifically help him. He'd been a golfer his entire life, even a young professional. He was returning to the game after a lengthy hiatus. In his mind he was, like me, a strong young golfer in a less co-operative older man's body. He was my perfect guinea pig, but I'll let him tell his own story.

Simon

I never reached Peter's great heights. My comfortable level was playing for my home county, Wiltshire and winning the occasional club championship. The thing was, I loved the game and still do. I love the people you meet, the fresh air and the magnificent courses dotted around the British Isles and beyond.

Serious illness in the late noughties kept me away from the game for eight years. On my return, I sought out my local pro, a good friend and renowned as a good teacher. It seemed the ideal opportunity to eliminate all the bad habits I had accumulated over the years.

On seeing me hit half a dozen shots he turned and said, "You play golf the elegant, old-fashioned way. It's lovely to watch but how do you want to play from now on, the old way or the new way?"

Never one to shirk a challenge, I naturally responded by asking to be taught the new way. My lessons were bearing some fruit, I seemed to hit the ball further and at times better, but I found consistency illusive and I simply couldn't put a decent score together. The 'new way' was turning out to be too physically demanding. My handicap had reached a lofty 13 and was still heading North but worst of all, I wasn't having fun.

What I needed was a coach who understood the challenges age and infirmity can bring, so I went online and searched for, 'best golf coaches in the UK'. Peter Dawson's name came up and he had a golf academy only a few miles from my home.

I recognised the name and thought to myself that, not only had Peter been a top player, he was the right age to empathise with my struggles learning to cope with the limitations

and frustrations of advancing age. I immediately booked myself in for an assessment and it was a revelation. Here was a man who had played at the highest level and understood exactly what it was like to be a back-niner! Peter had thoughtfully adapted the 'walk he walked' in his professional playing days to improve players like me.

We hit it off straight away. Peter was direct and kept everything simple. On that day, I left behind all notions of contorting myself into positions that ran the risk of doing permanent damage. Quite the opposite, he had some very clever and different ideas that made it easier for me to swing with wonderful results. He didn't discard my elegant 'old way', nor did he try to shoehorn me into the 'new way' we both knew I couldn't achieve. If you like, he, introduced a hybrid – or in my case, one might say, a rescue.

My handicap quickly dropped to a comfortable six. He's even managed to salvage me from 'the curse of the old golfer' – my short game. Under Peter's expert and easy to understand tutelage even that's improved.

I hope that this book inspires you to new heights of golfing achievement, but if not, I promise you'll be entertained by his many wonderful quotes, stories and anecdotes.

One of the finest sights in the world:
the other man's ball dropping in the water
– preferably so that he can see it
but cannot quite reach it
and has therefore to leave it there,
thus rendering himself so mad
that he loses the next hole as well.
– Henry Longhurst

Important technical information

Those who remember me from my playing days will know I always played left-handed as can be seen from this photo of me with my 70's garb and hairstyle.

The majority of golfers (about 90%) play golf right-handed. With this in mind, it made sense for the instruction pages in the book to feature me playing and demonstrating the swing right-handed.

THE ESSENTIALS
The four golfing musketeers

Your best chance of applying the club correctly is to start your swing from a position which makes the correct impact probable.
– John Jacobs

What are the essentials?

If you set up correctly, there's a good chance you'll hit a reasonable shot, even if you make a mediocre swing. If you set up to the ball poorly, you'll hit a lousy shot even if you make the greatest swing in the world.
— Jack Nicklaus

Pick up pretty much any golf instruction book and there they are, *The essentials*, usually taking pride of place at the beginning because, as Jack Nicklaus rightly points out, they really are the essential starting point for every successful golf shot however good the swing.

Whatever their technique, good and great players all have one thing in common, they respect the essentials and adopt an excellent address position with good posture.

I like to summarise these essentials as follows:

Grip – controls the club face

Posture – dictates the plane of the swing

Stance/alignment – influences the direction of the shot

Ball position –affects the trajectory

These are the basics that every golfer needs to apply if they hope to reach their full potential. Equally when players are not playing well it is almost certain that they will be doing one of these four essentials wrong.

That said, we back-niners need to adapt. As we get older our bodies lose their flexibility making it increasingly difficult to swing the club as we once did.

Later in the book I will be giving you ideas of how these essentials can be tweaked slightly but in order to do so successfully it is important that we back-niners respect and apply these basic elements.

THE GRIP

Golf begins with a good grip.
— Ben Hogan

My advice is don't get too hung up on trying to achieve the perfect grip, unless your grip is causing problems that affect your swing. As long as your hands are working together as one solid unit there's no need to change, leave well alone.

There are, however, certain things that are important to remember when taking your grip, these being:

- whatever grip you adopt the hands must work together

- always hold the club in the base of your fingers, not your palms, that's where the power and the feeling comes from

- keep hold of the club with all eight fingers throughout your swing

- your grip should remain light, relaxed and even

- check your grips with your pro to make sure they are the right thickness for you.

How important is the correct grip?

If this was another of those highly technical books that delve into the science and technique of golf, I'd be banging on about the importance of having the correct grip, but it's not. It's a book for us, the shall we say, more seasoned campaigner.

Whilst the way you hold the club is vitally important when you first start, after many years of playing the game we've all settled into a grip that, while not technically perfect, is comfortable.

It's also likely that your swing has naturally adapted to the way you grip the club, so as long as the hands are working together as one solid unit there's no need to change. My advice is leave well alone unless absolutely necessary.

Which grip is best for you?

I'm not going to waste too much time on which grip is best, I'm sure that all of us will at some stage have tried all three of the most common grips - the interlocking, overlapping (Vardon) and baseball grips.

The Vardon grip tends to be the most popular, however, those with smaller hands might find the interlocking slightly more effective whilst the baseball grip can create more hand action through the ball, which can produce a few extra yards.

Whichever grip you use, the most important thing is that it feels comfortable and enables your hands to work as one unit.

> *If people gripped their knife and forks like they grip a golf club, they'd starve to death.*
> — attributed to Sam Snead

What is the right grip pressure?

Grip pressure, not a flaw in technique, is the biggest factor when you are nervous. You unconsciously grip the club tighter, which keeps you from making a smooth swing with natural release. Keep your grip pressure light, and you'll be surprised how much your mechanics stabilise. – Ernie Els

Ernie Els makes it all seem so simple and he's absolutely right. Gripping too tightly causes tension not just in the hands, but up the forearms and into the shoulders preventing you from swinging freely.

So what pressure is correct when holding the club at address?

Some pros recommend that you imagine you're gripping an egg or a baby chick. Personally, I like to imagine I'm gripping a tube of toothpaste. As you can see in the images below, it's a lot more practical!

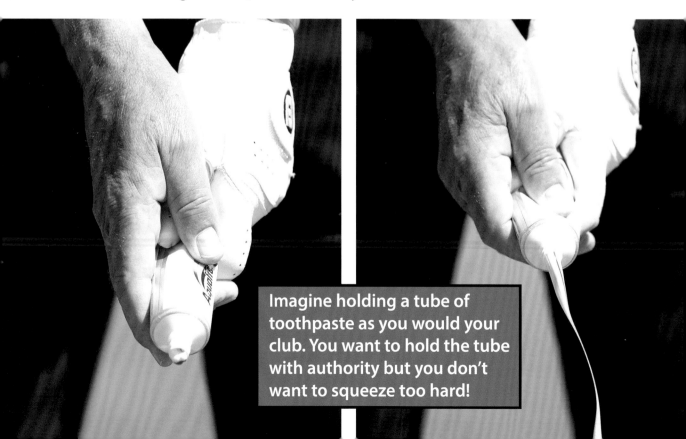

Imagine holding a tube of toothpaste as you would your club. You want to hold the tube with authority but you don't want to squeeze too hard!

Grip the club with your fingers not palms to maximise power and feel. Remember to keep hold with all eight fingers throughout the swing.

The baseball grip

Have you ever tried the two-handed (baseball) grip? This grip will give you just a little more whip with your bottom hand and may gain you an extra ten yards. Try it sometime, nothing ventured nothing gained!

POSTURE

> *Posture is all-important. There really is no excuse for standing badly at address.*
> — Justin Rose

Why is good posture so important?

Your posture basically dictates everything, especially:

- the plane and width of your swing in particular our extension through the ball

- our balance, rotation and the power you create.

How can we maintain our posture throughout our swing?

Having taken the time to adopt a good posture at address all this good work will be undone if you don't maintain that good posture throughout your swing.

Here are the important posture thoughts:

- keep your knees flexed throughout the swing

- keep your height

- maintain your spine angle

- keep your weight evenly balanced and on the balls of your feet

- let your eyes follow the ball on your follow-through.

The good, the bad & the ugly

Good posture is essential to the golf swing, just as good foundations are crucial to a building's construction.

Tom Weiskopf, a great player, was the perfect example of an excellent posture. In his heyday, Tom looked every inch a military man, shoulders back, chest out, head up and his swing mirrored the way he carried himself. Having played with him, I remember it well, it was most impressive!

Advancing age inevitably affects our posture and this in turn influences our golf swing. At address, it's imperative you adopt the best posture you can. A useful tip whilst playing is to walk between shots with your shoulders pulled back and chest pushed out in preparation for the next shot.

Great balls of power!

It's essential at address and throughout the backswing that your weight remains on the balls of your feet, never on the heels. When throwing a ball, you always have your weight forward because you get no leverage from your heels. This will give you a more dynamic and positive set up.

90%

Simon

When I returned to playing, I found that my time out had badly affected the essential factors of my golf swing. After such a long break and being in such poor condition, I found it difficult to take up a good posture so I did what many mature golfers do, I took the lazy option and went for comfort. This meant I didn't have enough room to rotate my body and create the free-flowing circle required for consistency and power.

My wrists tried to compensate for my hunched position and closed stance resulting in spectacular shanks, big pushes to the right and the occasional snap hook. Basically I didn't have a clue where the ball was going.

Peter soon set me straight. He made me realise how much I'd digressed, got me standing correctly, with better posture, good alignment and with the ball placed correctly in my stance. The results were instantaneous.

Even now, I can still relapse into my lazy posture, especially during the winter, so I've had to train myself to adopt a setup routine that consistently delivers a good posture and setup.

Peter also gave me insight into little tweaks that can help to generate more power, these I find invaluable and are included later in the book. I recommend you give them a go.

I always like to see a person stand up to a golf ball as though he was perfectly at home in its presence.
— Bobby Jones

Practice drills to improve posture and setup

Place club down the length of your back with your head touching the shaft.

Bend forward from the waist flexing your knees keeping your back pressed against the shaft.

Lower your head to bring the ball into vision keeping your knees flexed and weight evenly distributed.

The Peter Thomson set up drill

Take stance standing up straight with your club held out in front of you in your leading hand.

Lean forward from your waist until the club is resting behind the ball.

Complete your grip by adding the bottom hand. Flex your knees and you are good to go.

It's no use having lessons to correct your posture, grip and swing if your alignment is poor.

I've witnessed quite a few pre-shot routines over the years and my experience is that the alignment of most amateurs is poor.

Players often complain to me about losing their balance during the swing. This can be caused by bad alignment and the subconscious kicking in to try to get the club back on track turning the whole thing into a comedy of errors.

Whatever alignment technique you use, (I detail a few for you to try later in this section), always:

-        align your shoulders with your target

-        follow the same set-up routine

-        take a full practice swing visualising the ball flight

-        as Harvey Penick famously said, 'take dead aim'.

The critical alignment factor is the shoulders.
— Jack Nicklaus

Align your shoulders with your target

It's not unusual to watch experienced golfers meticulously aligning their feet or holding a club parallel to their hips and believing they're perfectly aligned when in fact they're far from it. It's actually the shoulders that need to be correctly aligned, not the feet and hips, these can point a few degrees either side of the target line.

Follow your personal routine

Whatever technique you adopt, the only hard and fast rule is to find a method that works best and is most comfortable for you. Our will to win is important but the will to prepare is vital too.

Whatever approach you take to alignment, you must apply the same hard and fast routine to every club. The key here is practice. When practicing, always pick out a target rather than just hitting aimlessly down the range. Place a club or a direction stick on the ground in line with the target. If done diligently, it will become second nature.

Practice your intended swing

Your pre-shot routine should always include a full practice of the swing you intend to make, including visualising the flight of the ball. This will programme you in advance, clearing the path for your subconscious to take over for the actual shot.

As Harvey Penick advised, always '*take dead aim*'* at a spot on the fairway or the green, refuse to allow any negative thoughts to enter your head and swing away.

Beware! Being sloppy causes poor shots. Always ensure your alignment is correct and feels right. An extra few seconds spent lining up is far better than time spent looking for your ball!

*Harvey Penick co-authored, *The Little Red Book* with Bud Shrake. It became the biggest selling golf book ever published.

Four popular alignment routines to try

Stand directly behind the ball, point the club out straight down the line of the shot and visualise the flight of the ball.

Place the clubhead behind the ball, square it to the target, take your stance in line with the clubhead.

Line yourself up to the target by holding a club across your body.

Choose a spot three feet in front of the ball and in line with the target. Line up to that spot.

BALL POSITION
Keep it simple

DRIVER

HYBRID

IRONS

TARGET LINE

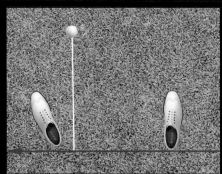

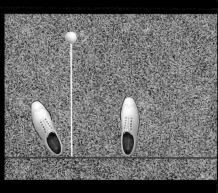

Why is the ball position so important?

So, there you are standing over the ball, taking dead aim at the target. Your posture and alignment are perfect, you've followed your setup routine and you're ready to pull the trigger. There's one final check you must make before sending the ball on its way. Is the ball positioned correctly in your stance?

The old myth has it that the shorter the club the further back the ball should be in your stance, which leads to playing the most lofted wedges almost from the back foot. This is far too complicated. I like to keep the ball position as simple as possible so it can be easily repeated.

The ball position influences your alignment. If too far forward in your stance, your shoulders will be too open causing you to swing from out to in, whilst too far back then the opposite will apply.

The positioning of the ball and feet influences the trajectory of your takeaway and downswing. Too far back in the stance, for example, can cause too steep a takeaway and downswing. Equally, the position of the ball and feet also enables the hit to take place at the right moment in the swing, for example, on the up with a driver or fairway wood and on the way down for a wedge.

It all sounds a bit complicated. The images on the following pages explain it better.

The main thing is keep things simple!

KISS – Keep It Simple, Stupid
Originally it was the acronym for a design principle noted by the U.S. Navy in 1960 but really good advice for anyone who tries to complicate golf.

Driver – the ball is positioned opposite the front instep to hit the ball on the upswing for increased top spin and distance.

Fairway woods – position the ball opposite the front heel. For tight lies or more control place the ball slightly further back in your stance.

Hybrids – these clubs have replaced long irons for most of us, place the ball in the same position as you would for those clubs.

MID-IRON

All Irons and wedges – position the ball some three or four inches back from the front heel.

9-IRON

As the club gets more lofted, the back foot moves nearer the front foot, narrowing the stance and naturally setting the ball closer to the back foot.

WEDGE

It's the back foot that moves, not the ball position.

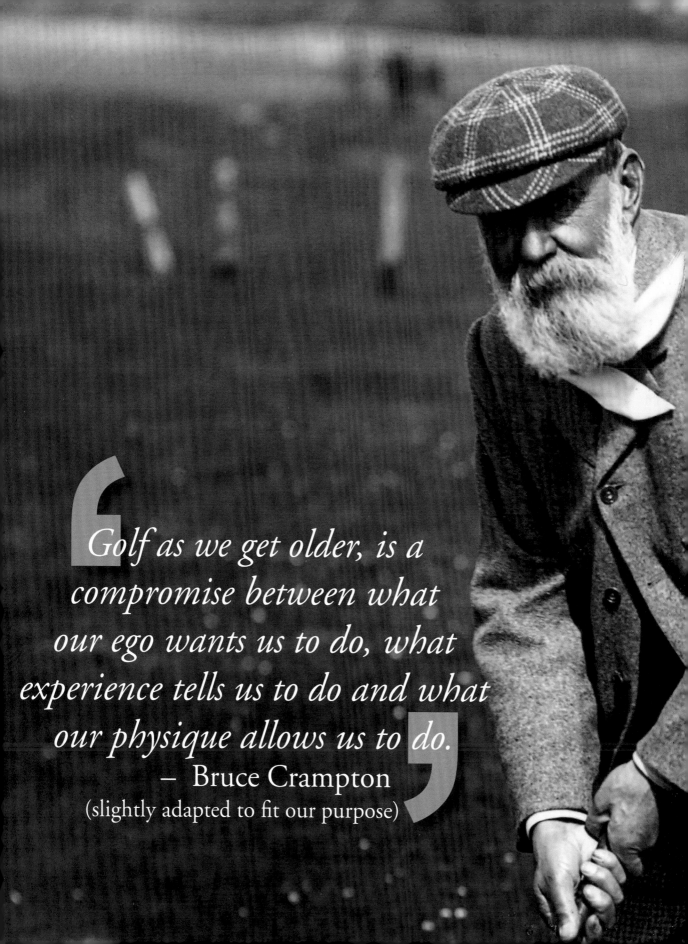

'*Golf as we get older, is a compromise between what our ego wants us to do, what experience tells us to do and what our physique allows us to do.*
— Bruce Crampton
(slightly adapted to fit our purpose)'

GETTING ON WITH GETTING ON A BIT

This is the important part of the book.

Having brushed up on 'The essentials', we can get down to what this book is really about, how to adapt the golfing essentials to our ageing physiques.

This chapter examines ways to help you recover those lost yards.

In the singles in the 1977 Ryder Cup, I was drawn against Don January, a gentleman and true veteran of the game. A former USPGA champion, Don was 48 at the time and definitely on the 'back nine' of his golfing career, though he went on to win 22 US Senior Tour events. To my delight, I overcame him 6 & 4.

After the match, Don and I sat down for a chat and a cup of tea. I had been impressed with Don's classic swing and told him so. His response has stuck with me ever since. He told me that as he got older and his physique and body changed, it required him to adjust his swing every two or three years. Considering the trend had always been to work hard to create your swing and then maintain it, this idea seemed very radical at the time.

A few years on, I realised Don was speaking good old common sense.

Why back-niners need to adapt

Reduced strength – as we get older our strength diminishes, we must adapt to get the distance we need, especially off the tee.

Limited flexibility – our range and ease of movement reduces, especially our ability to turn, exacerbating our reduced strength.

Bad habits creep in – the two points above cause us to subconsciously seek distance in other ways such as snatching the club away in the misguided belief that a faster and harder backswing generates speed.

So it comes down to making the most of what we have, what we know and how we use our experience.

THE DRIVER

With the exception of the putter, the driver is the most used and important club in the bag. It can also be the source of our greatest expense as not only is it usually the most expensive club in our bag but also the cause of most of our lost balls!

On the following pages, we look at a few ways you might be able to recover some of those lost yards without losing your accuracy.

usual posture with your shoulders back, your head held high, no hunching over the ball

knees flexed

ball teed slightly higher, opposite the front foot

weight on balls of feet

stance fractionally wider than shoulders with back foot slightly drawn back

50%

50%

Address position

start takeaway in one piece with shoulders, arms and hips all turning together

back knee remains flexed

be sure to maintain your width on the takeaway

weight still on balls of feet

60%   40%

Takeaway

back knee
remains flexed

top arm remains
straight

weight still
on balls of
feet

weight
transfers onto
front foot
at start of
downswing

75% 25% 40% 60%

The swing

head and chest start turning towards the target

bottom arm straightens

follow-through as far as possible with head and chest now fully facing target

30%   70%   10%   90%

Driving to success

I'm regularly asked who impressed me the most technically during my playing career. It's always a difficult question to answer as I played with so many great players.

At the 1977 Open at Turnberry, forever remembered as, *'The duel in the sun'*, I had the good fortune not only to play with the eventual winner, Tom Watson, in the first two rounds but then another Tom in the third round – the 1973 winner Tom Weiskopf.

Tom Weiskopf was renowned for his technically beautiful golf swing. In my opinion it was better than that and of all the great players his swing still stands out the most for me. I remember watching Tom in awe especially his driving, the perfect combination of aggression and grace.

Today's examples would be players such as Ernie Els, Adam Scott and Justin Rose and pretty much all the top lady professionals. These great players are all great drivers of a golf ball, they have wonderful rhythm and balance that will see them through into their senior golfing careers.

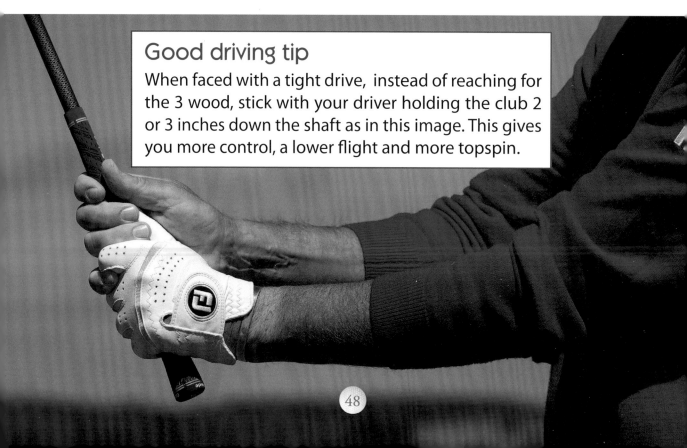

Good driving tip

When faced with a tight drive, instead of reaching for the 3 wood, stick with your driver holding the club 2 or 3 inches down the shaft as in this image. This gives you more control, a lower flight and more topspin.

Bernhard Langer wins the 1993 Masters – the last major won using a wooden-headed driver

It's extraordinary how dramatically golf equipment has evolved over such a short period of time as rival manufacturers battle for supremacy of the fairways. This is epitomised by the driver and the golf ball both of which have been the subject of huge investment over the past 30 years.

The photo below shows how the driver has progressed. The wooden-headed club was in use in the 1970's when I was playing pro tournaments. Just look at the size of the head compared to the modern metal one.

Through the years of experience I have found that air offers less resistance than dirt.
— Jack Nicklaus

Drivers past & present

A different type of driving experience

On my first visit to Nigeria we experienced a military coup!

On landing at Lagos International airport we were separated into three groups, to play in 36 hole events in different regions of Nigeria. My group took an old DC3 plane to Benin, (rumour was it had been used in the Biafran war).

The coup happened whilst we were in Benin. A curfew was imposed, so we had to return to our accommodation by 4pm. Returning from playing, a couple of us encountered a local soldier on a push bike coming down the road with a machine gun slung across the handlebars. The roads, not uncommon to ours these days, were full of potholes. Twenty metres ahead of us he hit a series of them, triggering the firing of a burst of bullets! Fortunately, the gun was pointing away from us towards the opposite side of the road and a parked white Peugeot car took the full force.

After the event, which I won, we had to return to Lagos for the main event, the Nigerian Open staged at the Ikoya Country Club in Lagos. Due to the coup, there were no flights so the organisers arranged cars and coaches to return us to the capital. I still remember vividly three of us with clubs and suitcases being shoe-horned with the driver into a Peugeot estate and the tremendous heat, (no air conditioning in those days). It was a very long journey.

It quickly became clear that the driver either had a death wish or had bet heavily on getting us to Lagos first. As we crested the top of many a hill we would see the road descend into a valley below to a SINGLE lane bridge at the bottom, (space for one car)! On each occasion and much to our horror, he took on the challenge to cross the bridge ahead of the oncoming vehicles! I can still hear the screams of three young budding Jack Nicklaus's in the car. We were lucky, we crossed the bridges in one piece, however, our eyes were drawn to the numerous cars and coaches that hadn't.

During the journey our driver decided to take the opportunity to visit a relative in a village he must have thought was close to the highway. We turned off the tarmac and proceeded down a dust track for a considerable distance into the bush. Kidnapping and robbery were a distinct possibility in the risky political climate of the moment.

Upon arriving in the village the driver got out of the car leaving us sitting there to reflect on our situation. It was midday and already very hot but I don't think the heat was responsible for the few extra beads of perspiration when the three of us realised the potential mess we were in!

Some fifteen minutes later the driver returned and we were on our way again. Such was life on tour in those days.

LESS IS MORE

LESS back   MORE through

Over the years I've seen so many players whose poor follow-throughs are a consequence of what has gone before. Their backswing being based on the misguided belief that a bigger shoulder turn on the way back means more distance. It doesn't, it usually means more chance of something going wrong.

Here are two ways in which you can influence and improve your follow-through with slight changes to your stance and ball position.

1. Try opening your front foot

Open your front foot by up to 30%. This will enable you to achieve a wider, fuller follow-through.

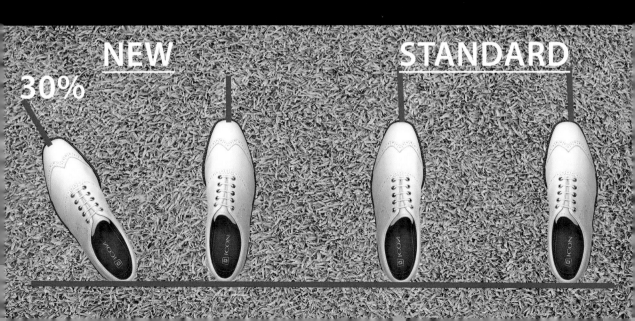

30%

NEW

STANDARD

2. Place the ball further forward

When driving, if you place the ball two or three inches further forward in your stance, your follow-through will naturally be wider and fuller as more weight has to transfer onto your front foot. This weight shift gives greater forward momentum, leading to more power and clubhead speed. It might feel a bit awkward at first, but try it.

There is life after impact

Most back-niners can't swing back as fully as they once did but can still complete their follow-through so this is where they need to concentrate their energies. A bit like throwing a ball, you can actually lob it with a minimal backswing because the power is all in the follow-through.

People often try to tell me that golf isn't a natural game. Nonsense. When you throw a ball do you practice the movement? No, you just pick the ball up and throw it under-arm in one natural movement and without a thought. You don't stand there, painstakingly line yourself up and then start thinking about the angle of your hand and arm as you draw your arm back to throw. Your arm simply goes back and through and nine times out of ten goes straight where you intended.

The images on the opposite page compare the movement and position on the backswing and follow-through when you throw a golf ball, swing one-handed and then two-handed.

Need I say more?

It isn't as easy as that of course, it never is! If it was this would be a very short book. But it does simplify the golf swing to the bare essentials and the closer you can get to this action the better your swing and the results will be.

The beauty of this exercise is that you can easily throw a ball in the garden so next time you have a spare five minutes go outside pick up a ball and throw it. Then repeat it with your eyes shut and try to imagine you are swinging a golf club.

In golf as in life it is the follow-through that makes the difference.

— Dr Seuss

Hitting the wall
(Opening and closing the door)

This is a brilliant exercise you can do anywhere, all you need is a wall. It's an extension of what the old pro's used to refer to as *'opening and closing the door'* when describing the golf swing. The images on the page opposite, show how simple and effective this exercise can be.

The idea is very straightforward, it replicates the position you should be in when you strike the ball. Stand with your leading foot against the wall, take your normal backswing and return to hit the wall making sure that your chest is facing the wall on impact as in the bottom photo. This enables you to feel the correct position of the shoulders and chest at impact and the way the head automatically moves forward with them, it does not stay still!

The proximity of the wall highlights any incorrect movements that you make during your backswing as you will find it difficult, if not impossible, to return to the correct impact position. This can be seen opposite where Simon's poor posture creates a flat backswing and a poor impact position.

Returning to the old pro saying and analogy - the arm is the door and the spine is the door-hinge.

Note: Why not try to make this movement part of your pre-shot routine or at least picture the movement during your practice swing. It should help improve your position at impact.

This exercise is also brilliant for the short game.

'Nothing is particularly hard if you divide it into small jobs.
– Henry Ford'

Good posture
at address

Poor posture
at address

Head remains
still, back knee
remains flexed

Poor posture
causes head to
move and a flat
backswing

Full impact
position as
the whole
body rotates
forward

Poor posture
and flat
backswing
make it impossible
to achieve the
correct impact
position

The big finish

Most of us were brought up on that old saying passed down from generation to generation – *'Keep your head still, young man'.*

DON'T!

At the risk of repeating myself, a full follow-through is simply not possible unless the head moves forward and follows the ball. How can we possibly maximise the momentum of our follow-through if the centre of our swing is stuck where the ball started from?

Look at the photos below. See how my head and shoulders follow the ball enabling me to get right through the ball, whereas Simon's head has failed to follow-through, holding back his forward movement and preventing him from extending through the ball. This makes a plethora of bad shots likely.

If you need reassurance, there are some classic examples such as great champions, Annika Sorenstam (93 professional wins) and David Duval (The Open 2001), who always looked like they were lifting their heads as they hit the ball. They weren't, their heads were simply following the ball to maintain the momentum of their swings.

Another great example is our old friend Gary Player. He would regularly walk after the ball to ensure that he hit it with his full weight. Now that's worth a try, although I suggest you try it on the practice ground first.

Try walking after the ball

I've seen videos of pros on the driving range throwing their clubs after the ball as they complete their swing. This is a practice routine to help them achieve the big finish.

It isn't something I'd recommend as it could be very costly although I'm sure your club pro would see the financial benefits!

Next time you're practicing, imagine throwing the club after the ball without letting go, it will help you extend your follow-through.

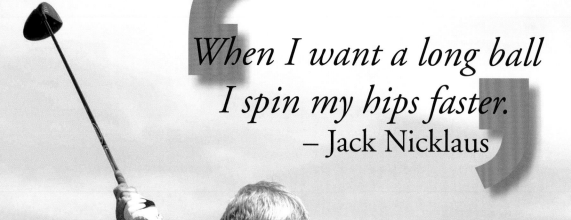

*When I want a long ball
I spin my hips faster.*
– Jack Nicklaus

Creating power
with your hips

GET HIPPY

What is the best hip turn for you?

The modern golf swing is much more physical than when I was playing the tour.

It requires a 90° shoulder-turn on the backswing, turning hard against the resistance of hips that only turn about 20°. The tension this creates causes the lower half to coil and uncoil like a giant spring generating enormous amounts of energy through the hitting area, many refer to this as *the coil*.

For most back-niners this is simply too physically challenging so we need to find other ways of creating *the coil*. On the following pages are five ways that can help you achieve this.

A quick word of advice, try them on the practice ground first and don't try all five ways at the same time!

*Reverse every natural instinct and
do the opposite
of what you are inclined to do,
and you will probably come very close
to having a perfect golf swing.*
– Ben Hogan

1. Try turning your back foot outwards at address

At address, turn your back foot slightly outwards as in the image below, this helps your hips turn back more freely but be careful not to overdo it as it will restrict your follow-through.

STANDARD

NEW

30%

TARGET

2. One piece takeaway

Start your backswing by turning your hips and shoulders together into the flex of your back leg.

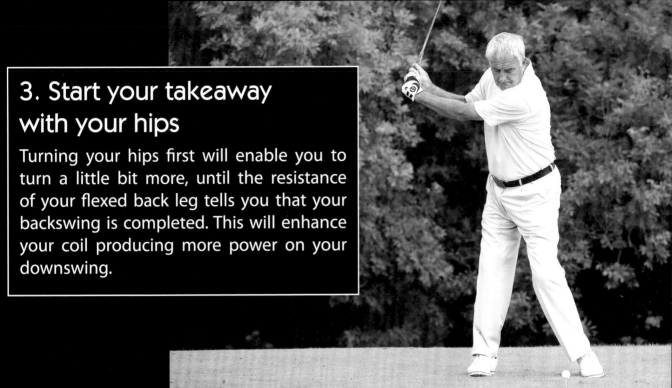

3. Start your takeaway with your hips

Turning your hips first will enable you to turn a little bit more, until the resistance of your flexed back leg tells you that your backswing is completed. This will enhance your coil producing more power on your downswing.

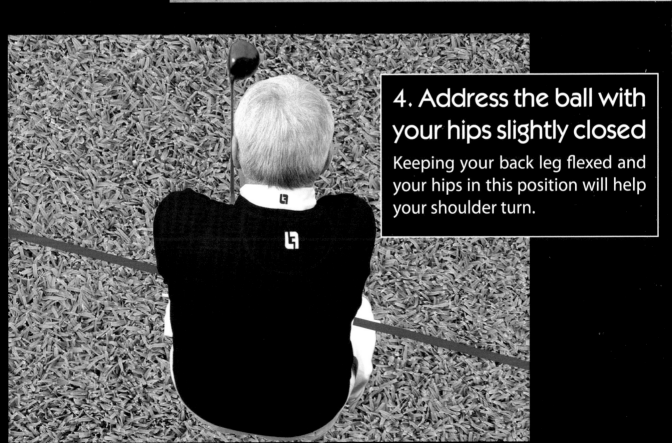

4. Address the ball with your hips slightly closed

Keeping your back leg flexed and your hips in this position will help your shoulder turn.

5. Back foot behind

Take your normal stance and then withdraw your back foot approximately six inches. This will give you a better hip turn which in turn will make the coil easier. Remember to keep the back knee flexed.

THE
TARGET

Give your swing a lift

A number of golfers think that lifting their front heel on the backswing is a deadly sin and the heel should remain firmly on the ground throughout. Tosh!

Keeping the front foot on the ground throughout the backswing can easily impair the backswing and actually lead to a reverse pivot and other nasties. The golf swing is a chain reaction, so if by turning the hips the heel wants to lift, let it.

Stand and deliver!

How to improve consistency and increase power through your address position

> *Be sure to put your feet in the right place and stand firm.*
> — Abraham Lincoln

Width of stance

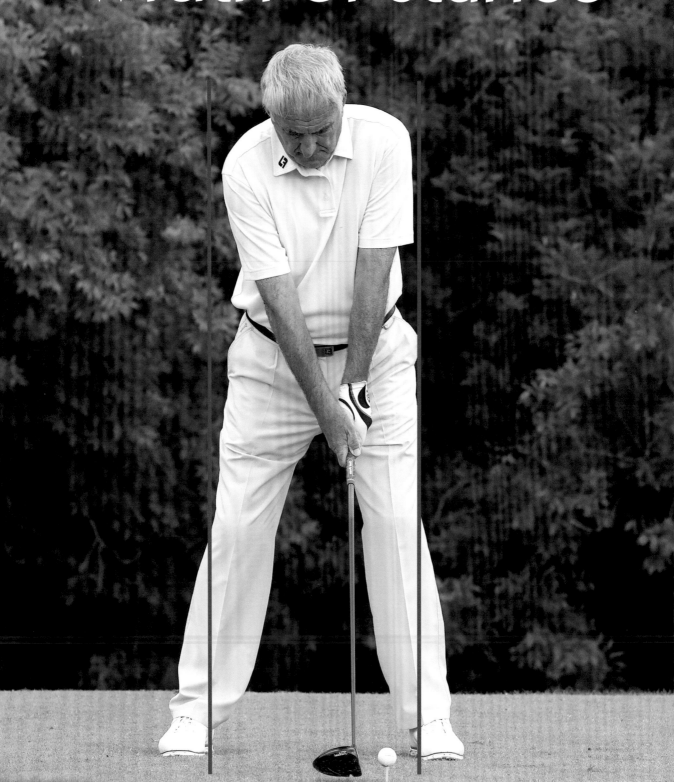

Why is the width of stance so important?

The images in, *The essentials* section on pages 38 and 39, demonstrate the ideal ball positions for the different clubs showing the ideal stance for a mid-iron as being roughly the width of the shoulders. For some reason, however, as we get older, we seem to think our shoulders are getting wider and wider!

The width of your stance is important as it dictates the amount you can turn, your weight transference and your balance.

We're all different with different physiques and swings and a stance that works for one may not work for another. Overleaf is a tried and trusted exercise to help you work out the best width of stance for you.

For every action there is an equal and opposite reaction.
– Newton's Third Law

How to work out the right width of stance for you

Next time you're out practicing, using a 6 or 7 iron, hit a few balls with your feet together and gradually widen them until you feel you're in a position that gives you the best and most unrestricted turn.

The other benefit of practicing these shots with your feet together is it helps with your balance, rhythm and establishing the correct body rotation.

The reverse pivot and how to avoid it

Too wide a stance not only restricts your turn but can lead to a reverse pivot and the variety of poor shots it causes. Below, Simon perfectly demonstrates the reverse pivot whilst I show you how to avoid this highly destructive and remarkably common fault.

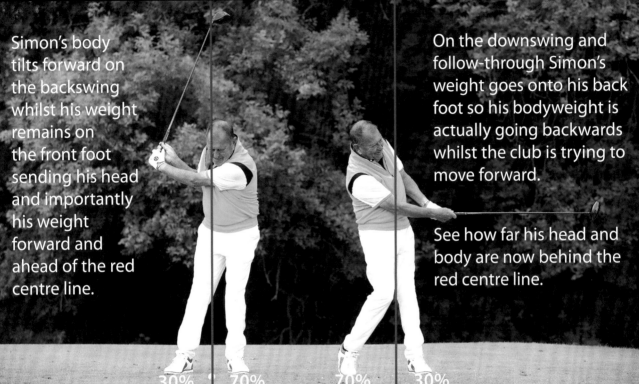

Simon's body tilts forward on the backswing whilst his weight remains on the front foot sending his head and importantly his weight forward and ahead of the red centre line.

On the downswing and follow-through Simon's weight goes onto his back foot so his bodyweight is actually going backwards whilst the club is trying to move forward.

See how far his head and body are now behind the red centre line.

30% | 70%   70% | 30%

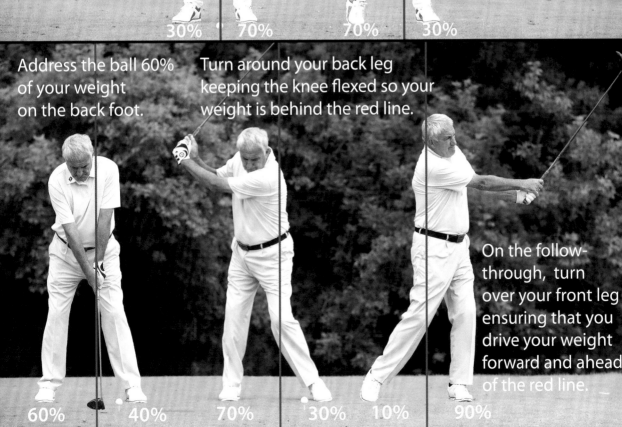

Address the ball 60% of your weight on the back foot.

Turn around your back leg keeping the knee flexed so your weight is behind the red line.

On the follow-through, turn over your front leg ensuring that you drive your weight forward and ahead of the red line.

60% | 40%   70% | 30%   10% | 90%

The magic circle

I like to think of the golf swing as a circle where the chest acts as the hub that everything rotates around.

Oh, how I wish it was that simple!

For us back-niners, such full movement is now beyond most of us physically and this causes a loss of turn and power. To overcome this, we need to find a better way to transfer our weight, I like to refer to this as creating an extended circle of power.

...how to create the
extended circle of power

Extending your circle of power

This creates a freer, more powerful swing that takes the stress off the lower back, which is great for us bad back sufferers. You can achieve this by shifting virtually all your weight onto your back foot on your backswing and then reversing that shift down and through the ball on your follow-through.

In the sequence below, you can see how my body and weight shifts from one side of the red centre line to the other as I turn back and through.

A great example of this was Curtis Strange, US Open Champion in 1988 and again in 1989. The more I play with a back that's refusing to pivot, the more convinced I am that this technique should be tried out by all of us elder statesmen/women.

Practice drill

Set yourself up with a pair of alignment sticks stuck in the ground either side of your stance.

Make sure that your weight is on the balls of your feet and that your back knee is flexed.

On your backswing, turn back transferring your weight on to your back leg making sure that it doesn't move on to the outside of your back foot. Your hips should virtually touch the sticks as in the images below making sure that you turn and don't sway.

Warning!

Be careful not to sway. Always rotate over your back foot on your backswing and front foot on your follow-through.

Backswing

- shoulders turned as far as possible

- hips almost touching sticks

- body weight now transferred onto back foot

- spine angle remains straight.

Follow-through

- like throwing a ball, the weight moves from back to front foot as your hips and chest rotate through the ball until they are well ahead of their address position (red line) with the hips almost touching the front stick

- spine remains straight to ensure no swaying.

ROLLING
ROLLING
ROLLING!

How copying the top tennis players can give you more topspin and more yardage off the tee.

Tee the ball higher and opposite your big toe.

Take your normal stance then pull your rear foot back six inches.

To hit the ball a long way we need fast clubhead speed at impact to compress the ball. It is alas a fact of life, that as we get older we lose the muscles and rotation required to hit the ball a long way. Though what we lose in carry can be made up for with extra roll.

How can you hit the ball with the extra topspin needed to create this extra roll when the ball hits the fairway?

One technique used successfully by a number of back-niners is based on the way that tennis players achieve more topspin on their forehand shots.

Tee the ball a little higher than usual, a third of the ball above the driver face, moving it forward opposite the front big toe. Withdraw the back foot some six inches.

Having done these three things, the result will be to hit the ball on the upswing with an in to out swing creating more topspin with a slight draw.

FAIRWAY WOODS

With age we use our fairway woods far more often so playing them well is increasingly important.

When hitting from the fairway you must feel you're sweeping the ball off the surface, never try to lift it, leave that to the loft of the club.

- sweep the ball off the surface

- if the ball is lying tight use a 5 wood

- grip a little shorter for control and lower ball flight

- ball position slightly further back than the driver.

The swing

As with the driver, it's important to maintain your height throughout to give your swing the width it needs to sweep the ball away.

The ball is forward in the stance, opposite the front heel, so the ball can be swept from the grass on the upswing.

Warning!

If the ball is nestling down slightly the great temptation is to blast away with a 3 wood and at impact try to lift the ball into the air with your hands.

Don't!

Take a more lofted wood or even a hybrid and sweep the ball away.

When playing a fairway wood from a downslope remember that the slope will reduce the loft of the club and the ball will fly lower. If the slope is a concern take a more lofted club such as a 5 wood or hybrid. The important thing is that your swing goes with the slope and you sweep the ball away.

Useful tip

The fairway wood is a lovely option when faced with a long fairway shot where you need control and accuracy, especially in windy conditions. Gripping down the club one or two inches will bring the ball slightly nearer in your stance making your swing fractionally steeper, producing lower ball flight with more control. It's almost like having an extra club in the bag.

I almost never hit a shot all out, and I make a conscious effort to swing my long clubs just as I do my wedges. Keep this in mind when hitting your fairway woods.

– Ernie Els

HYBRIDS

Welcome to your new best friends!

Whatever you wish to call them; hybrids, rescues, utility clubs or as the celebrated Mr Alliss refers to them, *'The Gentleman's Persuader'*, these clubs were invented just for us back-niners. They offer us more adaptability and with practice, a club not just for those difficult shots that previously required a long iron but also for playing out of the semi-rough, chipping and even long bunker shots.

In short, having one of these clubs in the bag is an absolute must for all back-niners.

Why are hybrids so much easier to hit?

The image says it all but for those who like to have a more scientific explanation:

Hybrids have a larger clubhead that allows manufacturers to position the weight lower and further back, creating a lower centre of gravity which helps get the ball in the air more easily. This, and its design, in particular the deeper and more rounded sole, produces a club that's easier to use and far more forgiving.

Which hybrid is right for me?

Manufacturers offer hybrids with lofts going from 14° all the way to 32° and beyond. It can be a bit confusing knowing how they equate to the old iron so here is a table to give you an idea of the equivalent iron and hybrids:

Hybrid loft	Equivalent iron
14° - 16°	1
17° - 19°	2
19° - 21°	3
22° - 23°	4
24° - 27°	5
28° - 31°	6
32°+	7+

The swing

One of the most frequent questions I'm asked is, *'should I swing my hybrid the same as my fairway wood or my 5 iron?'*

The rather bemusing answer I often give is simply, yes.

After all, a hybrid is both. It's the length of a long iron but the clubhead is more like the shape of a fairway wood.

The swing is therefore dictated by the design of the clubhead, the length of the shaft and the position of the ball in your stance. When swinging, imagine you're sweeping the ball away as you would a fairway wood and the ball position, (slightly further back in the stance), will create a slightly downward swing and a shallow divot.

See the swing arc below.

From the rough

It's a rough game and we're surrounded by the stuff!

The clubhead design makes them the perfect choice where distance is required from the rough or semi-rough although common sense should always prevail on club selection.

From fairway bunkers

Subject to the same common-sense approach to club selection, the clubhead design makes the hybrid the perfect choice for the long distance fairway bunker shot unless the lie and the lip of the bunker dictate otherwise.

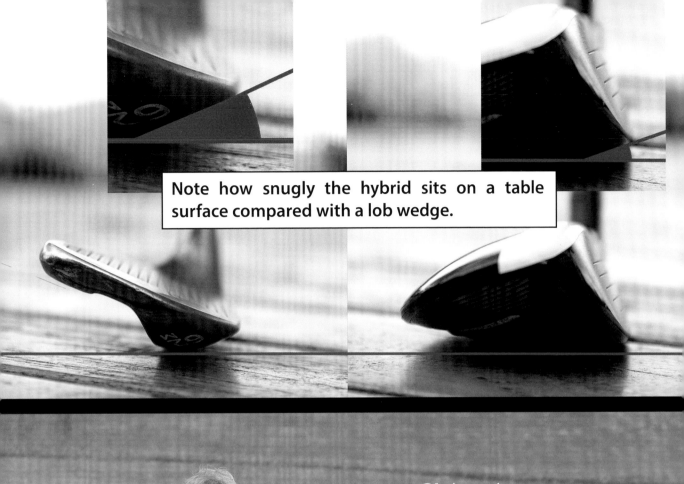

Note how snugly the hybrid sits on a table surface compared with a lob wedge.

Chipping

The deep, rounded sole makes hybrids perfect for the chip and run shot.

Play the shot with your weight fractionally on the front foot, gripping the club just above the shaft for more control. During the stroke keep the clubhead moving smoothly.

Use the grip that feels most comfortable and produces the best results for you. After all this shot is all about feel.

MID-IRONS

I like to think of the mid-irons and mid-iron play as the scoring shots.

There's nothing better than that lovely feeling of a wonderfully struck iron and watching as it heads straight at the target. We back-niners can even see them land!

The key to these shots is rhythm and control. For me, the best example of this was when I played with Tom Watson in the first two rounds of The Open, at Turnberry in 1977. Tom's rhythm throughout remained constant and it was fantastic to watch. He adapted his shot selection to his rhythm, by shortening or lengthening his grip, to give him the control he needed to achieve his historic victory.

Tom still swings it the same today.

How irons have developed

Historically, all irons were forged from a flat piece of metal pressed into shape to create a bladed clubhead. In the old days, no two 7-irons came out the same but modern casting processes have enabled manufacturers to produce clubs with consistent properties, although even now the system isn't completely foolproof. The casting process first used by Ping and now by most manufacturers, has made it possible to make clubs out of harder metals enabling them to distribute the weight better around the perimeter of the club. This peripheral weighting creates a larger sweet spot with the result that an imperfect strike is less disastrous. Cast or forged? Go with whatever you're happy with.

Modern iron design has made it easier and quicker to get the ball in the air, this has resulted in a gradual reduction in lofts. For example, the loft of a 7-iron has decreased from 40° to 30° over the past 40 years, and is now the same loft as the 5-iron I was using in tournaments in the 70's!

Hence today's 7-iron goes further than it's predecessor. This, in turn, has created the need for a greater variety of wedges and today most people's bags include the likes of an approach or gap wedge, sand wedge and lob wedge with lofts ranging anywhere between 48 to 64 degrees.

Comparison of men's iron lofts over the years

	1960's – 70's	1970's – 80's	1980's – 90's	1990's – 2000's	2000's – 10's
1-Iron	17	17	16	16-17	N/A
2-Iron	20	20	19	18-20	N/A
3-iron	24	23	22	20-21	17.5
4-iron	28	26	25	23-24	20.5
5-iron	32	30	28	26-27	23
6-iron	36	34	32	30-31	26
7-iron	40	38	36	34-35	30
8-iron	44	42	40	38-40	34.5
9-iron	48	46	44	42-44	39
PW	52	50	48	46-48	44
SW	56	56	55	55-56	54

The swing

- maintain the same swing and posture which each club

- hit down taking the ball first, then a small divot

- don't scoop the ball

- always maintain the same rhythm

- don't force these shots

- take care to maintain a nice rhythm and if necessary, take one club more and grip down the shaft.

The first patent for a steel shaft was made in 1910 by Arthur F Knight.

It took 10 years for the USGA to legalise the use of steel shafts.

It wasn't until 1930 that the R&A followed suit.

In 1931, the first major championship was won by a player using steel shafts – Billy Burke who won the US Open.

In 1969, Frank Wilson of Shakespeare Sporting Goods, invented the graphite shaft and since the late 1980's it's been the popular choice for drivers and fairway woods and is now becoming increasingly popular in the irons, especially with the senior players.

To find a man's true character play a round of golf with him!
– P G Woodhouse

WRIST BREAK

As back-niners, our bodies are unable to turn as fully as they once did, our swings shorten costing us power and distance in the process. Here are a couple of ways to overcome this by creating greater wrist break.

Although our position at address automatically produces a natural degree of wrist break during our backswing, we can increase this by starting our backswing with our wrists.

In the sequence below you'll see that my wrists are breaking quicker than normal though importantly the top arm is remaining straight throughout the backswing. This provides me with greater clubhead speed whilst retaining the width of my swing.

A simple method to achieve more wrist break is to lower your hands at the address position. This creates a greater, natural wrist break angle at the very start of the backswing. Another little exercise for your next visit to the practice ground.

Warning!

With either method, be careful that your forearms don't roll as you break your wrists. In the images below, Simon shows us perfectly, how not to do it!

Simon has broken his wrists, in doing so he's turned his left hand over and as a result his backswing is too flat and narrow. This must be avoided at all costs.

My advice is to try this first on the practice ground.

Playing from slopes

Few shots are played off completely flat lies. The most important thing when hitting any shot off a slope, is to understand what effect the slope is going to have on your shot. Here are some quick rules of thumb.

Uphill and downhill lies

In the images below, I've attached a magnetic alignment tool to the face of an iron and then tilted the photos to show how uphill and downhill lies affect the trajectory of your shots.

Downhill lies – these send the ball lower, adding top spin. Take a more lofted club and land the ball slightly shorter to allow it to roll out.

Uphill lies – the opposite applies with the ball coming off the clubhead higher so the ball stops quicker. Aim to land these shots nearer the hole. Also consider taking a slightly less lofted club.

Important things to remember:

- weight always favours the lower foot
- shoulders and hips are always parallel to the slope
- ball in middle of stance
- the club must follow the slope – this is especially important for downhill lies, when you mustn't try to scoop the ball.

Ball above and below feet

Again I've tilted the images to show how the slopes influence our shots, the red arrows show the effects on the alignment of the clubhead.

Ball above feet – there's a tendency to pull shots from these lies which creates a little more run on the ball, allow for this when taking aim.

Important things to remember:

- grip the club approximately two inches shorter
- ball middle of stance
- weight favouring toes.

Ball below feet – there's a tendency to slice the ball off these slopes, allow for this when taking aim.

- grip the club as long as possible
- ball in the middle of your stance
- flex your knees slightly more than usual
- weight favouring heels.

For both these shots try to eliminate as much leg action as possible, letting the top half of your body do the work.

The punch shot

One of the few advantages we back-niners enjoy when playing in the wind is that, because our clubhead speed is reduced, we tend to get less backspin on the ball making the flight of our shots lower and less affected by the wind.

Modern technology has specifically created equipment designed to get the ball airborne faster through the clubface grooves, the dimples on the ball and peripheral clubhead weighting. We can't eliminate these factors but we can reduce their influence.

To keep the ball lower, all we need to do is slow the speed of the clubhead down – with age and a slower swing we're already halfway there!

Address the ball normally but with more weight on the front foot resisting the temptation to put the ball further back in your stance as this can cause too steep a downswing and an open clubface at impact. Swing fully and smoothly.

A good tip is, instead of trying to hit a mid-iron or hybrid 150 yards into the wind, go down the shaft on a 3 or 5 wood, swing smoothly just trying to sweep the ball off the surface, don't hit down.

40%   60%   40%   60%   30%   70%   10%   90%

Life on tour

The start of it all

How did I start playing golf? It all started because my dad had a stroke in 1962 aged 47. His doctor advised him to take up a sport that would give him some gentle exercise. Being in his late forties, the options weren't many and living as we did on the edge of Scarborough South Cliff Golf Club in North Yorkshire, the answer was obvious. Golf became the focus in our family. I was 12 at the time and would caddy for him whenever possible, as well as a few of his more affluent friends to make a few shillings. After a few months of witnessing some pretty poor golf I thought I would see if I could do better.

In those early days I would borrow dad's clubs, jump the fence and play a few holes before being chased from the course by irate members. It quickly became clear they knew where I lived and I had to join the club. My dad was left-handed so I learned to play that way round, which was a pain as there were so few left-handed clubs for sale in those days. Golf superstores, eBay and online shopping didn't exist - especially in North Yorkshire!

I still recall dad taking me by steam train to Manchester to visit Lillywhites to buy my first ever set of clubs. It was quite an adventure and a very long day. Finally having my own clubs meant there was no stopping me and my dad and I chased each other down to single figure handicaps.

Being a junior member in those days only cost a few pounds. Somehow my parents found the money, like a great number of children, I was unaware of the sacrifices my parents made for me. I remember them convincing me that they preferred eating bread and jam sandwiches for tea whilst I was treated to something more nutritious.

In addition, I was challenged with a speech impediment that prevented me from speaking until the age of seven and I didn't start school until I was eight. As a result, I spent my school years playing catch up, failing miserably I might add. Golf gave me a great escape and improvement came rapidly with lots of practice.

I couldn't ask my parents for the money for my golf equipment, they worked all the hours God sent in their shop for very little profit, so whenever there was a competition I would wander out onto the course in search of lost golf balls, often scrambling down the cliffs next to the holes that ran parallel to the seashore. These were steep, high and damned dangerous!

Looking back, I shudder in disbelief at the fixes I got myself into when trying to reach that white shiny Dunlop 65 or Slazenger + golf ball. Many was the time I would lose my footing, literally grabbing hold of a clump of grass at the last moment to save me from a 200 foot fall. Phil Mickelson is blissfully unaware how close he was to being the first left-hander to play in the Ryder Cup!

In his later years my father would recollect those days, telling me how proud he and my mother were of what I had achieved. In my mind I had achieved very little, I never felt I had repaid them.

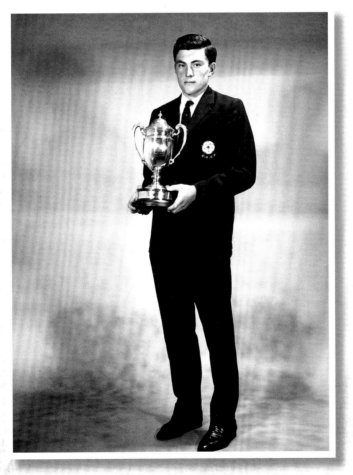

A young Peter Dawson after victory in the Carris Trophy in 1968

The caddie holes out!

During my early days on tour, the Dutch Open was played on a course where the 18th hole was a dog-leg with a blind second shot over a high sand dune some 100 yards from the green.

In those days players that missed the cut for the final day were permitted to caddy for a fellow professional to help each other keep expenses down.

On one particular occasion, one of the pros who'd missed the cut was caddying for his best mate in the final round. An early starter, the player was having a rare day when everything was going right. He'd played the front nine in 30 and needed a par at the last to break the course record.

It was before the days of large crowds and blanket TV coverage so members and guests interrupted their lunches to witness the great feat. The player's second landed in the middle of the green coming to rest on the back fringe close to the clubhouse veranda.

A heated discussion then began between player and caddy as to the line of the putt. In the end the caddy grabbed the putter and duly putted the ball up to the hole much to shouts of astonishment from the spectators.

'Oh Mijn God, the caddy has putted the ball!'

The crowd was unaware this had all been planned. After hitting his approach from behind the mound and unseen by everyone around the green, the player had taken the caddy's bib from his great pal and put it on, he then picked up the bag of clubs put them over his shoulder and handed the real caddy his putter. So when the two walked onto the final green, to much applause and excitement, the crowd was completely unaware they had swapped roles so when the 'caddy' holed out it had in fact been the player the whole time!

No rules were broken and it livened the conversation of the members and guests as they returned to their lunches.

With today's crowds and television cameras all over the place such fun is a thing of the past, besides I can't imagine the European Tour accepting such outrageous frivolity from two of its members!

Never give up!

Fred How is not a name you'll know. He was a former POW in Singapore during WWII and my caddy during my better days on the tour. Like many young men in the war, life had dealt him a bad hand. I mention him because in one tournament, which was going badly, I had virtually given up all hope of qualifying for the final round when he came out with the statement, *"You know if I had given up all hope I wouldn't be here now"*. To this day I remember dear old Fred.

A player who epitomised that 'never say die' attitude more than anyone was Gary Player. When Gary started out on the tour, many people told him to go back home to South Africa because he wouldn't make it, referring to his slight physique and the flaws in his technique.

Oh how they underestimated his immense spirit and how hard he was prepared to work. I don't think it ever crossed his mind that he wouldn't make it. Sixty or so years later, winner of 9 majors and 165 tournaments worldwide, Gary is one of the all-time greats and a wonderful ambassador for the game of golf.

The last tournament I played on the South African circuit was at the Kensington Golf Club in the Johannesburg suburbs and I was due to fly to Manila to partner Nick Faldo in the World Cup immediately afterwards.

I made a terrible start, five over par after nine then dropping another shot on the tenth, I wasn't happy. Walking down the 11th fairway I muttered something to Lizzy, my wife, who gave me short shrift, basically telling me to pull my finger out and stop whinging! Suitably chastened, I followed her instructions and a sprinkling of eagles and birdies saw me home in 31.

I was now in the groove and the next day went out in 31 before coming home again in 31 shots. Three halves of 31 in succession, 14 under par for 27 holes and leading the tournament by a shot!

In the final round I partnered the eventual winner Gary Player, whilst I faded to third. Although slightly disappointed not to have won, had I given up on that first day, I wouldn't have flown to Manila feeling a little smug. I hope Fred would have been pleased with me, I know Lizzy was!

Life on tour can be a pain in the backside

In 1976, I played in the Nigerian Open in Lagos. During the tournament I'd developed what I thought was a large boil on my backside. The flight home was most uncomfortable and after a couple of days I informed Lizzy enough was enough. The irritation and pain had become so unbearable that I was intent on bursting it! I closed myself in the bathroom. To say the least, I was rather amazed when a large white maggot appeared!

I quickly picked up the wriggling thing and popped it into a small plastic container then, with all speed shot off to our local surgery. Even in those days surgery receptionists had the well-trained skill of transforming themselves into brick walls – *'No booking – no appointment. Read the sign!'* Her squat stance, square shoulders and furrowed brow left me in no doubt that there were strict protocols, she was in charge of them and I was not going to be seeing any doctor under her watch!

Well, two could play that game. I inwardly grinned as I handed her my little container as an apologetic peace offering. One look at my offending friend and I was straight in.

Steve, our GP and friend, had served in the army in Africa. He'd seen these little chappies many times. I vividly remember him dismissively flushing the container's resident down the loo. All evidence of my horror was casually lost forever!

Steve explained that the nasty little grub was the larva of a botfly. They lay their eggs on other insects like flies and mosquitoes that in turn transmit them to humans. In the African bush, he went on, the most effective solution was to strap a chunk of raw meat over the 'boil' to cut off the air supply. When the maggot was suffocating it would migrate into the raw meat. Alternatively I could have simply put up with the pain for six to eight weeks when it would drop out of its own accord and turn into a fully blown botfly. The trick was that it was essential that the entire larva be extracted as any bits left could cause infection and any number of real problems. I was lucky and out of danger.

Travelling and problems with customs

During the winter months I would play a few pro-ams or small tournaments in California. On one such occasion I was returning from the USA with my then brother-in-law John Garner (Ryder Cup 1971 and '73), we were both contracted to Ping at the time and had visited their factory to pick up our new equipment ready for the upcoming European circuit.

Coming through the 'nothing to declare' channel at Heathrow, John and I were pulled aside by the customs officials and escorted to separate interview rooms. Our golf bags were stripped, the clubs counted and then the interrogation began. *Why were we bringing sets of expensive golf clubs into the country through the green channel? Were we trying to evade paying import tax?* Hours passed whilst we tried to explain we were pro's on the European Tour and the clubs were the tools of our trade.

Meanwhile our wives had no choice but to leave us at the airport wondering how it all might turn out in the end.

In desperation, I even suggested that the officials could keep the clubs in store until the following week and I'd pick them up on my way to the Italian Open. I'm not sure what convinced them in the end, but at around 5pm we were released and our wives returned to the airport to retrieve their very frustrated husbands intact and still with the tools of their trade!

Apparently, in the early 70's, the dollar was on a high and it wasn't uncommon for golfers to holiday in America return with a new set of clubs they would then sell at a handsome profit often unashamedly placing an ad on the golf club notice board right under the club pro's nose. We were just caught up in it all.

This story also reminds me of when I was an assistant professional in Johannesburg in the early 70s, golfers from what was then Rhodesia would stuff their dollars down the shafts of their clubs and then ask us in the proshop to snap each club in half to retrieve their money.

On another occasion, returning from the French Open, my wife and I were accompanied by a good friend of ours Craig Defoy, a fellow tour professional. Needless to say, two big tour bags and all the suitcases meant we had an overloaded car.

We were stopped by suspicious customs officials, who seemed determined to pull anything from the car that could possibly be removed, even the back seats! No politeness from our part saved my lovely new car. Naturally nothing was discovered and much to my relief the officers put the seats, spare wheel and everything else back, which I later found out they didn't have to do.

Thomas Bjørn

I spent three years as coach to the Danish squads. This consisted of around 150 days of the year working over there with some very talented youngsters. Each country has its own lifestyle and language which makes my job interesting. The team was willing to work hard and listen, although my regime of clean shoes and no jeans was a little difficult to stomach by some of the players.

At the end of the three years I wrote my final report on the team to the Danish Golf Union Committee. There were a number of players wanting to turn professional, including one Thomas Bjørn. I reported that Thomas could stand on any practice ground of any professional tournament and look the part. During my time coaching their squads, he was the one player who stood out both for his work ethic and his will to succeed, there was plenty of Danish grit there!

I wrote that with hard work and a little good fortune he would win professional tournaments and participate in the Ryder Cup. I also thought him capable of winning The Open when he was at his best, which he came very close to doing at Royal St Georges in 2003. He has won 15 tournaments worldwide to date and not only played in three Ryder Cups but captained the winning team in 2018!

I wish I had kept a copy of that last report.

Shot-maker extraordinaire – Lee Trevino

In the first two rounds of the 1978 Open at St Andrews, I was drawn with two previous winners, Bob Charles, the first left-hander to win a major (1963), and Lee Trevino (1971 and 1973). Bob, a gentleman, got on quietly with his job, Lee talked incessantly to himself, his caddy, and the crowd but was always respectful of everyone around him, me I was in the middle!

I think everyone acknowledged that Lee Trevino was one of the greatest shot makers of our generation, and I had the privilege of having a ringside seat! Lee and I would also be drawn together in the third round. He played shots with enormous talent and fantastic imagination, and what really impressed me was the fact that he was playing these shots under great pressure.

I specifically remember the 11th hole, it's a par 3 some 170 yards in length. Right in the centre of the approach to the green is a really treacherous bunker named 'Strath'. Invariably the tournament committee placed the pin right behind the bunker. On the first day, I remember Lee aiming a 4 iron well left and slicing the ball around the bunker, the following day he did the opposite aiming well right and hooking an 8 iron onto the green. At no time did the hazard come into play. On both occasions I had a 5 iron in hand wondering how I would get the ball high enough and long enough to carry the bunker and stop before it went over the back leaving me with an almost impossible chip.

After the third day's play had finished, I threw my clubs in the boot of my car and exclaimed to Fred, my trusted caddy, in a very depressed way that I would never be able to play golf like that! Oh I could do it on the practice ground and during practice rounds but I never had the talent or courage to do it in a tournament.

With today's equipment those wonderfully imaginative shots of Lee Trevino are sadly a thing of the past. Today it's all about length and putting.

Before the days of sports psychologists

After winters spent plying my trade on the Australian and South African tours, plus the occasional trip to America, my first European tournament would be the Madrid Open staged in early April at the lovely Puerto De Hierro Golf Club.

It was always an eagerly awaited event as it was the start of a new season and the chance to visit a great city with wonderful restaurants. I remember well Casa Paco for their steaks and Casa Botin for their suckling pig, the latter claiming to be the oldest restaurant in the world dating back to 1725.

One year in the first round, I was drawn to play with a past Amateur champion who had recently turned pro with much expected of him. In those early days he possessed a quick temper which on this occasion cost the host venue a few pesetas.

We had reached the 12th or possibly 13th, a difficult par four with a tight drive played from an elevated tee. He teed his ball up close to the tee marker to get a better angle, gave it a quick swing sending the ball off at right angles into the trees. On completion of his follow-through, without pausing, he took a backward swipe and dismantled the tee marker, a yellow shiny plastic ball of a type we still see today.

Bits of plastic went flying everywhere followed by a few choice words on how he didn't like that particular tee shot, how the angles were all wrong and he couldn't get a visual image of the required shot.

We arrived at the same tee the next day with both of us a couple over par and needing a strong finish to qualify for the weekend. Again he teed the ball up close to the marker and had a couple of slow, relaxed practice swings. With deliberate preparation, he checked his alignment, grip, and ball position whilst glancing down the fairway a few times checking it was still there. He drew a gentle intake of breath and was ready to go. Despite this careful preparation, there followed a very fast swing full of anxiety and fear and another disastrously wayward shot. This time there was a slight pause at the end of his follow-through, before he took an almighty backward swipe at the replacement tee marker.

Unbeknownst to anyone, the seemingly identical yellow replacement sphere had one minor but very important difference from the broken original, this one was made out of concrete.

This time the tee marker won the day. A lovely persimmon driver at speed is no match for concrete!

Adverse weather

I have to thank the UK's bad weather for winning the Double Diamond Scottish Open in 1975. Out early on the second day, I was playing the front nine at Turnberry into a breeze that as we got further out blew much stronger. Turnberry goes virtually straight out, turns and barring 12 and 15, the back nine heads straight back home again.

I had managed to get to the turn in a couple over par when the wind really started to blow and used the strong following wind to my advantage coming back in one under par for a 73.

It was the best score of the day by far and I leap-frogged the entire field. Being a 36-hole tournament I emerged as the winner. The money I won helped me start out on married life later that year. Over 40 years have gone by and that was a great investment, thanks Lizzy.

***

A couple of years earlier in 1973 the Scottish Open had been held at St Andrews, again I benefited from bad weather. I was new to the tour having won enough from my African ventures and smaller assistant events in Yorkshire to start life with the big boys.

I still remember how awestruck I was when I first played St Andrews. The very first tee shot has two fairways to aim at, the first and 18th, no problem until on the first day you are drawn to play with Roberto De Vicenzo, winner of 230 tournaments worldwide including the Open in 1967, a colossus of a man, an absolute gentleman too! This Yorkshire lad was truly out of his depth, that first fairway with its acres suddenly became the width of a lawn mower. Funny what nerves do to you.

I just made the last day and was due out first just after 8am. An odd number qualified so I went out with a marker. I used to like playing quickly and we were at the turn in under one and a half hours.

St Andrews is designed on a narrow strip of the Fife coast. The first 7 holes go straight out to a loop of four holes which criss-cross before the 12th heads back home. As I reached the furthest point of the course the tide turned bringing high winds that blew me all the way back in. Returning on the back 9 I could see my fellow competitors struggling to cope with the front nine. I had started tied for 50th, my 72 was the best round of the day and rocketed me up into a tie for 14th!

I can still recall the fun of sitting having breakfast at 11.30 back in the hotel watching on TV as my name moved up the leaderboard minute by minute.

Good old Scottish weather!

Hole in one

Fancy having a hole in one in The Open at Royal Birkdale! Then heaving a heavy sigh on realising there was virtually no-one watching.

That was me in 1976. It was the 3rd round and I was out early, about 9am. The course was still silver with morning dew and it was far too early to warrant cameramen or live commentary. It was just me, my playing partner, our caddies and a handful of keen fans in the stands to bear witness. I approached the 4th tee with 5-iron in hand. My shot felt sweet as it whistled off the club face and our early birds were all too happy to let me know where the ball had finished. I was equally thrilled to have rewarded their enthusiasm!

These days a hole in one wins you a flash car or something equally eye-popping. In 1976, I proudly received a jeroboam of fine Champagne and a weekend at the luxurious Turnberry Hotel in Ayrshire. The Champagne was thoroughly enjoyed although I never got to take that weekend in Scotland. Regrettably my tour commitments kept us from going as Lizzy still enjoys reminding me!

Perhaps I should give a certain US President a ring!

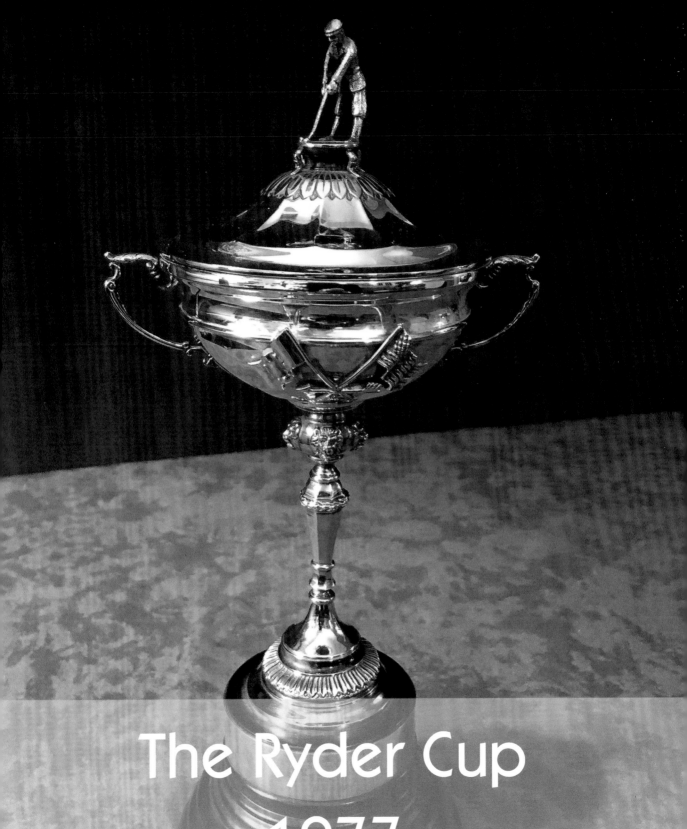

The Ryder Cup
1977

The Ryder Cup of 1977 is my most treasured golfing memory and without doubt the one golfing achievement that people remember me for, depending of course on their age. You could say it was my fifteen minutes of fame.

The Cup was played that year on home soil at Royal Lytham. It was the final time our team would be made up solely of players from Great Britain and Northern Ireland. The continent of Europe led by the extraordinary Seve, would join forces with us in time for the next event in 1979.

In the fourball and foursome matches I had the great fortune of partnering Neil Coles. Neil was a regular winner on the European tour, an 8-times Ryder Cup player, a stalwart of the tour.

In the Foursomes on the first morning, walking to the first tee I presumed Neil, as the experienced player, would take the first tee shot. No, I seemed to have been talked into taking it or was it a toss of a coin? I don't recall exactly which but I do remember Neil's words at the time *at least if you shank the tee shot it will stay in bounds* (referring to me being left-handed). This quote was still bouncing around in my head when the starter announced me as the player to take the opening tee shot on behalf of the Great Britain and Ireland team.

The first hole at Lytham can be described in professional terms as a fairly gentle par three, except of course for the bunkers surrounding the green, a number of trees, the railway line and out of bounds down the right – oh and the small matter of stands to the left and behind the green crammed full of spectators!

Nervously teeing the ball up, I had never before seen the head of a 5 iron look so small and so far away. By chance I hit a decent shot to the middle of the green and Neil was a little unlucky not to hole the putt. Seventeen holes later we lost a close match on the 18th green.

On the 8th green in the fourballs, Neil had a fifteen foot putt for a half, whilst my ball was only about three feet from the hole. Neil narrowly missed leaving me with the now much more difficult three-footer for a half. I like to think I held my nerve and holed out but sadly I can't remember.

In the crowd watching was Dai Rees, nine-time Ryder Cup player and five-time team captain. Afterwards he commented to me that in my situation he would have putted first as it's far harder to putt last especially when it's for the half. Over the years when coaching international squads I've passed that invaluable insight onto the players.

Bunker trouble in the Ryder Cup at Lytham

The United States team was strong and contained golfing greats such as Tom Watson, Raymond Floyd, Hale Irwin and the greatest of them all, Jack Nicklaus. We fought hard but in the end they were just too strong for us, triumphing by 12 ½ to 7 ½.

After the play and celebrations had finished we all returned to the hotel for the final dinner in the evening. Just below my room, one floor down and fractionally to the left was the suite and balcony of the American team. Every so often a member of their team would step out with the trophy in hand raising it to the crowd gathered below.

The previous evening I'd eaten something that had disagreed with me and the doctor on call recommended flushing out my system with some soda water, a couple of syphons were left over. During a lull in celebrations I phoned reception asking for an American player to come out onto the balcony with the trophy.

I had calculated the distance between floors and worked out that as soon as I saw the foot of the US player appear, if I let go with both syphons, I would hit the target a bit like in Grand Prix podium celebrations.

I waited, poised, both syphons at the ready. A leg appeared, both syphons were deployed sending two lovely jets of soda arcing through the air on a superb trajectory directly to where the American player would be standing with the trophy. Grinning with glee at my imminent success I suddenly realised who the US player was, none other than the greatest player in the history of the sport, Jack Nicklaus! I have to confess it was like watching a car crash in slow motion, I wanted to hide but deep down I was rather proud of myself.

A few minutes later there was a knock on the door and there stood Hubert Green and Dave Stockton with a bottle of champagne each. Sadly, these weren't for a celebratory drink, they pulled me out of the bedroom and sprayed me with the stuff, it stings the eyes I seem to remember!

In the evening at the dinner Jack Nicklaus approached me with a big smile, absolute gentleman and great sportsman that he is, he took the festivities all in the good spirit intended.

Quite often around the Ryder Cup date I'll get a call from a pub or golf club somewhere in the UK asking if I really was the first left-hander to have played in the event. Apparently I am a regular quiz answer although I have yet to feature on *Pointless*.

It's always great fun saying yes. Now of course and far more famously, there has been Phil Mickelson and Bubba Watson from the USA leaving me now just to boast that I'm the only European. It is still a nice accolade having been the first although a lot of people think it was Bob Charles.

The weekend before the Ryder Cup we had played the Tournament Players Championship at Foxhills in Surrey finishing on the Sunday. I had thrown the tournament away when only needing to par the last to win. Ironically the winner of the event was Neil Coles, my partner in the Ryder Cup.

After my disaster at Foxhills we returned home, packed the car and drove up to Lytham that same evening. At some point on the M6 motorway in Lancashire we were stopped by the police for speeding, as the officer looked around the car he enquired after the golf equipment in the back probably wondering if it was stolen. Naturally I explained where we were heading, it turned out he was a keen golfer himself and he let me off with a warning and a good luck message. We met up again at Lytham 4 days later when he turned up to watch me do my job after I had witnessed him doing his on the Sunday evening!

During the Ryder Cup I received a telegram from the bank manager of the Midland Bank at Filey in Yorkshire. A few years earlier I had asked him to grant me a loan so I could play the African circuit which at the time consisted of the Opens of Nigeria, Zambia and Kenya. In those days there were no big sponsorship deals from the likes of Nike and Callaway. We would either use our own money or borrow from a bank.

Fortunately, he loaned me enough to start out, and some four years later I was at Lytham, mixing with the likes of Tony Jacklin, Nick Faldo, Jack Nicklaus, Hale Irwin and Tom Watson. I can't remember the exact words but they went along the lines if ever I wanted another loan I knew where he was!

Golf is deceptively simple and endlessly complicated. It satisfies the soul and frustrates the intellect. It is at the same time rewarding and maddening and is without doubt the greatest game mankind has ever invented.
— Arnold Palmer

THE SHORT GAME

> *The only way to win golf tournaments is with the short game. Over half your shots out there are played from within 30 to 40 yards.*
> – Phil Mickelson

I make no apologies for the length of this section, it's a commonly accepted fact that well over 50% of all golf shots are played from within 80 yards of the hole and as our drives and long shots get shorter, we increasingly rely on our short game.

The key elements to a good short game are:

- strategy
- imagination
- feel.

All these come with practice and combine to give us the most important element of all.

CONFIDENCE!

Simon

My short game has been the part that I've found hardest to recover and it has let me down regularly since my return to playing. My eight-year break effectively reduced me to a gibbering wreck and my confidence was shot. I'd basically forgotten how to chip properly and this led to every example of bad shot – shanks, duffs, thins, you name it. If I was in a position to hit a bad shot, rest assured I found it. It was all too shamefully easy for me to be 10 yards from the green in regulation and take 6 more to hole out.

This section describes the common-sense approach Peter took to improving this part of my game.

Life is not a matter of holding good cards,
but of playing a poor hand well.
– Robert Louis Stevenson

30 TO 80 YARDS

Hold the vision and trust the process.
— Unknown

When I first started playing we only carried two wedges, a pitching wedge with a loft of about 52° and a sand wedge that was usually about 56°. These days, although the loft of the sand wedge is pretty much as before, a pitching wedge has much less loft, usually 43° or 44°.

The gaps are now filled by specialist wedges with lofts varying from 48° to 60° or even higher. Not only is the choice of loft greater than ever before but you can now even choose how much the clubhead bounces.

Bounce? I hear you say? Yes bounce, the technical term for how much lower the sole of a wedge is in relation to the leading edge. The diagram below shows how the bounce is calculated by measuring the solid blue area which represents the degree of bounce. But why? What's the point?

Different bounces are required because players' techniques can vary greatly, as does the type of shot. To find out what is going to suit you best, please ask your club pro. In the meantime here is a brief guide.

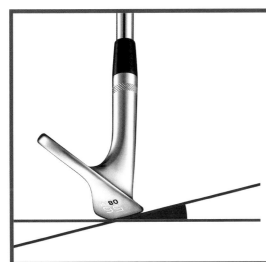

Low bounce
Ideal for shots from tight lies and firm turf conditions.

Standard bounce
The best all-round wedge for most conditions and all types of players.

High Bounce
Usually only available for higher lofted clubs, they're designed for play out of soft turf, heavy rough and soft sand.

We all carry at least three wedges in our bags these days. The individual lofts are very much down to personal preference. My pitching wedge has 43° loft so I've arranged the shorter clubs accordingly, carrying a 48°, a 52° and a 58°. These, I believe provide me with the perfect balance.

Whatever permutation you prefer, the aim is to get the ball as close to the hole as possible with imagination, feel and a good technique.

40%   60%

Address position

The essentials

Grip – the same as usual except slightly lighter and shorter for increased feel and more control.

Posture – usual posture adapted to the length of club with your shoulders back, your head held high and no hunching over the ball. Your weight should slightly favour your front foot with your knees flexed.

Stance – your feet should now be closer together caused by your back foot moving further forward and closer to your front foot. See *The essentials* on page 39.

Ball position – about three to four inches inside your front heel. The narrowing of your stance means the ball is in the middle of your feet.

Taking up your address position

The easiest way to get into the correct position at address is to address the ball with your weight evenly distributed – when doing so, your hands will naturally meet in the middle of your body. If you then slide your weight slightly forward (60%) onto your front foot, your hands will automatically follow and move slightly ahead of the ball. One thing influences the other.

The extra weight on your front foot should remain there throughout your swing and ensure that your wrists break a little earlier than usual on the backswing enabling you to hit down and take the ball first.

The Swing

Never force these shots and always try to swing the same, controlling the distance through club selection and moving your hands up and down the grip.

The key is control.

Backswing

- take the club back so your top arm is parallel to the ground
- keep your weight on the front foot
- knees remain flexed.

Follow-through

- follow-through slightly beyond the parallel with the rest of your weight transferring onto your front foot
- eyes and head follow the chest and shoulders through the ball to face the target.

40%   60% 30%   70%   10%   90%

30 YARDS IN

> *Perfection is attained by slow degrees, it requires the hand of time.*
>
> – Voltaire

Tom Watson famously chipping in at Pebble Beach on the 71st hole to win the 1982 US Open.
We are most grateful to Tom for giving us his personal permission to use this photo.

40%   60%

THE CHIP

Posture – good posture at address is essential for all shots especially chipping, this includes:

- head held high
- shoulders back
- bend from the waist
- knees flexed.

Grip – some players change their grip for chipping, anything goes really.

These shots are all down to imagination and feel so whatever grip you adopt, it should be light to maximise feel. Too many bad shots are caused by gripping the club too tightly. Remember the grip section and the open tube of toothpaste (page 27)? A good exercise when practicing is to close your eyes and work out what grip and pressure gives you the best feel.

Some players prefer thicker grips on their wedges as they feel it gives them better feel and helps restrict wrist movement. If it works for you, go for it!

Alignment – the alignment of the shoulders, hips and feet varies with the different types of shot however, the clubhead should always be aligned to the target.

Ball position – is in the middle of your feet for all shots.

Weight distribution – your weight should favour your front foot remaining there throughout the swing whatever the shot.

Chipping technique

- weight constant at 60% on front foot until after impact

- hands working as one unit, no flicking with bottom hand

- eyes follow the ball

- play the shot with imagination, picking the spot where you want the ball to land

- grip 2 or 3 inches down the shaft for more control

- legs remain quiet throughout the swing

- try to create a pendulum movement where the backswing is the same length as the follow-through.

40%   60% 40%   60%   30%   70%

Leg movement

In my experience, most poor chipping is caused by too much leg movement.

The images opposite show my leg movement during the chipping sequence.

You can see the leg movement is minimal throughout with the swing being driven solely by my arms and shoulders.

This is very important and on pages 142 and 144, I suggest a couple of good drills that can help you to practice hitting your shots with just the shoulders and arms.

It's good sportsmanship to not pick up lost golf balls when they are still rolling.
– Mark Twain

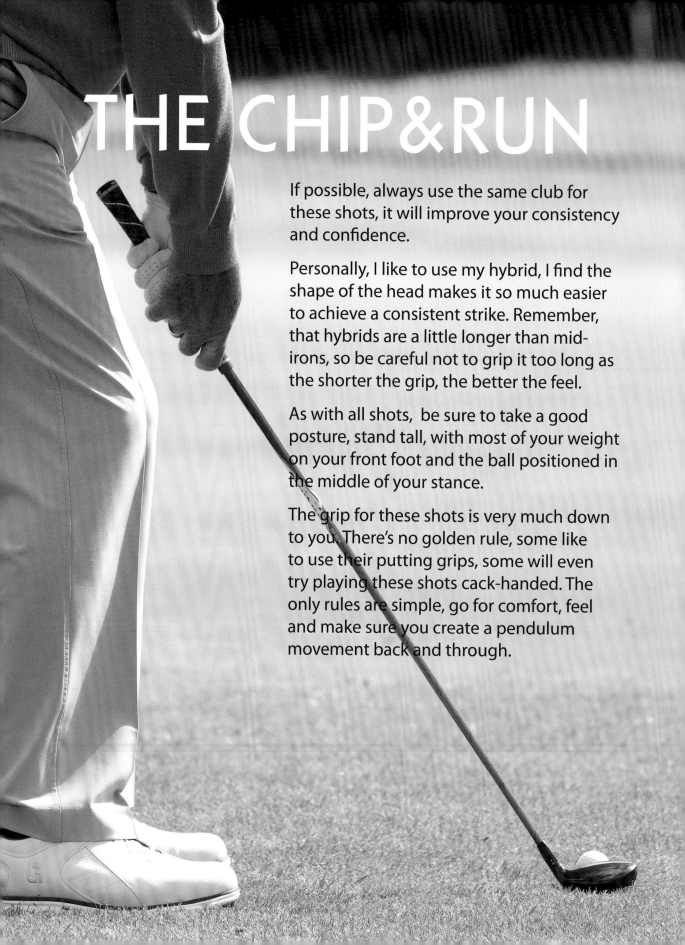

THE CHIP&RUN

If possible, always use the same club for these shots, it will improve your consistency and confidence.

Personally, I like to use my hybrid, I find the shape of the head makes it so much easier to achieve a consistent strike. Remember, that hybrids are a little longer than mid-irons, so be careful not to grip it too long as the shorter the grip, the better the feel.

As with all shots, be sure to take a good posture, stand tall, with most of your weight on your front foot and the ball positioned in the middle of your stance.

The grip for these shots is very much down to you. There's no golden rule, some like to use their putting grips, some will even try playing these shots cack-handed. The only rules are simple, go for comfort, feel and make sure you create a pendulum movement back and through.

Chipping from divots

Assess the depth of the divot. If it can be taken cleanly and there's nothing to go over, then the hybrid is ideal for this shot.

If however, the ball is sitting well down or there is something to go over, take a pitching wedge and play ball and turf at the same time.

Put more weight on your front foot to create the steeper angle of attack needed.

WARNING!

The temptation is to try and lift the ball with your wrists as Simon has tried to do and fluffed it completely.

DON'T!!

These shots are potential card wreckers and must be treated with care and commitment. Whatever shot you play, commit to it, hit through the ball and let the club do the work.

Bare lies

The more delicate shots around the green become increasingly troublesome for back-niners and isn't it always the way that when you have a good score going you find yourself faced with one of these delicate shots with the ball lying poorly, such as on a bare lie.

If there's nothing to go over, I advise you use a club with a flat sole that can sit nicely behind the ball such as a hybrid or putter, personally I favour the hybrid as it gives the ball a little more loft.

See how snugly the hybrid sits behind the ball

The problems really start when you have something to go over such as a bunker. The regular reaction of many a back-niner is simply to grab hold of their most lofted club and try to lift the ball up and over, usually with disastrous results such as a topped shot into the face of the bunker or one that carries over the bunker and shoots across the green usually with disastrous results. We've all done it!

Believe me, even the top players hate this shot. It requires imagination and a lot of common sense, especially with club selection.

The problem is that the design of the sole of the modern wedges, especially the most lofted ones, makes the clubhead bounce when playing out of these lies. That bounce needs to be eliminated.

So we're looking for a club that will give us the height we need but without creating bounce. Here are two options that are tried and trusted.

Method 1

Go for a less lofted club such as a pitching wedge, which has a sole with less bounce. Remember that, because it's less lofted, the ball will have a lower trajectory and roll further when it lands, so it's only really suitable where the bunker you're playing over is quite shallow and there's plenty of room to land the ball. Avoid this option when you're short-sided with little green to play with.

Method 2

Take your most lofted wedge, close the face slightly and address the ball towards the toe of the club as in the image below. See how much more snugly the club sits behind the ball eliminating the bounce. The ball will naturally come off the clubface slightly pulled and a bit lower, although this varies for each individual player, so as with many of these tips, practice it first!

IMPORTANT NOTE: Both methods require a normal stance and swing.

Uphill and downhill chipping

As explained on page 92, when playing these shots it's important to take into account the effect the slope will have on the trajectory and roll of the ball. Uphill slopes naturally increase the loft of the club sending the ball higher whereas downhill slopes do the opposite.

Posture – again, good posture at address is essential:

- head held high
- shoulders back
- bend from the waist
- knees flexed.

Grip – shorter grip for control. Remember to keep it light to maximise feel.

Stance/alignment

- slightly wider stance for more stability
- shoulders and hips go with the slope

Ball position – in the middle of your feet.

Weight distribution – your weight must always favour the lower foot, in other words the back foot on uphill shots and front foot for downhill.

The most important message is
DON'T FIGHT THE SLOPE!

Chipping with ball above feet...

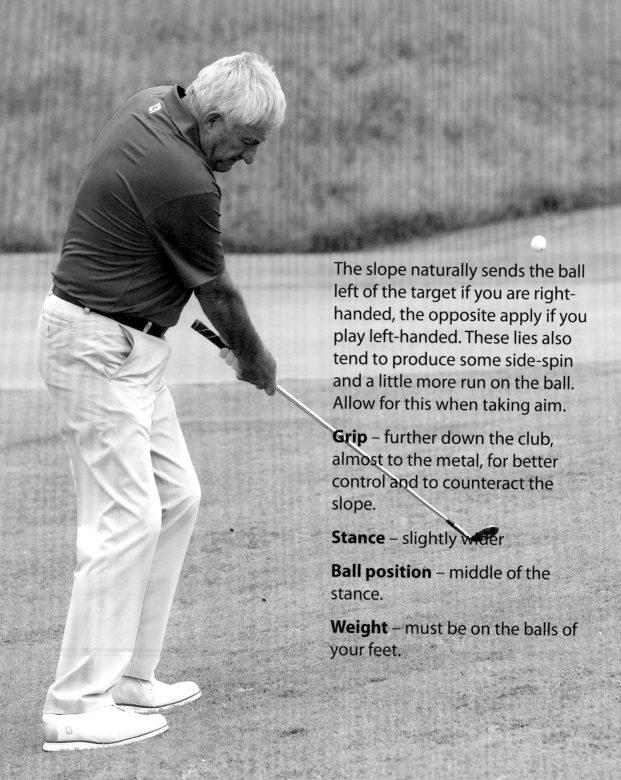

The slope naturally sends the ball left of the target if you are right-handed, the opposite apply if you play left-handed. These lies also tend to produce some side-spin and a little more run on the ball. Allow for this when taking aim.

Grip – further down the club, almost to the metal, for better control and to counteract the slope.

Stance – slightly wider

Ball position – middle of the stance.

Weight – must be on the balls of your feet.

... below feet

When the ball is below your feet, the opposite applies.

Grip – grip the club to it's full length.

Posture – flex your knees slightly more than normal.

Stance – slightly wider.

Ball position – middle of your stance.

Weight – must be towards the heels of your feet.

Warning! – if the slope is pronounced, there's a danger of the heel digging into the slope hooding the face in the process, so take care.

Chipping from the semi-rough

The ball tends to sit down with at least half of it below the level of the grass, cushioning the ball on impact, causing a loss of backspin and more roll when it lands. Use your normal chipping technique with slightly more weight on the front foot to create a steeper angle of attack into the back of the ball. Remember to allow for the extra roll.

Chipping from deep rough

The most important thing with these shots is strategy.

Your priority is always to get the ball out. Beware the grass wrapping itself around the hosel, closing the face at impact. To prevent this, open the clubface slightly at address and grip the club tighter at impact remembering to keep your weight on your front foot throughout.

As you would a plugged ball in a bunker, place the ball in the middle of your stance, attack the grass and create an explosion.

Shot selection around the green

The French refer to *System D* as a way of responding to challenges by adapting and improvising to get the job done. This could easily describe how we approach those little shots around the green when any club in the bag can be used, it is really down to personal preference and imagination.

Many golfers, favour the 60° lob wedge, their imagination tending to stop there. An old Scottish caddie once said to me, *"Why hit the ball so high laddie when a running 5 iron would suffice?"* Fast forward to today and he would probably advise a hybrid.

In certain circumstances of course, we have to use our most lofted clubs, for example, when having to chip the ball over bunker and rough, but except in those situations, why not play the percentages and hit the shot with the least margin for error.

Personally, I like and recommend the hybrid, it's ideal for those running shots. Being a straighter-faced club, you need a shorter backswing, which gives you more control. It's also more forgiving if you catch the ground before the ball as the wide sole tends to bounce rather than dig in. Below are some of the options at your disposal and how the ball acts with each club.

Lob Wedge

9 - iron

Hybrid

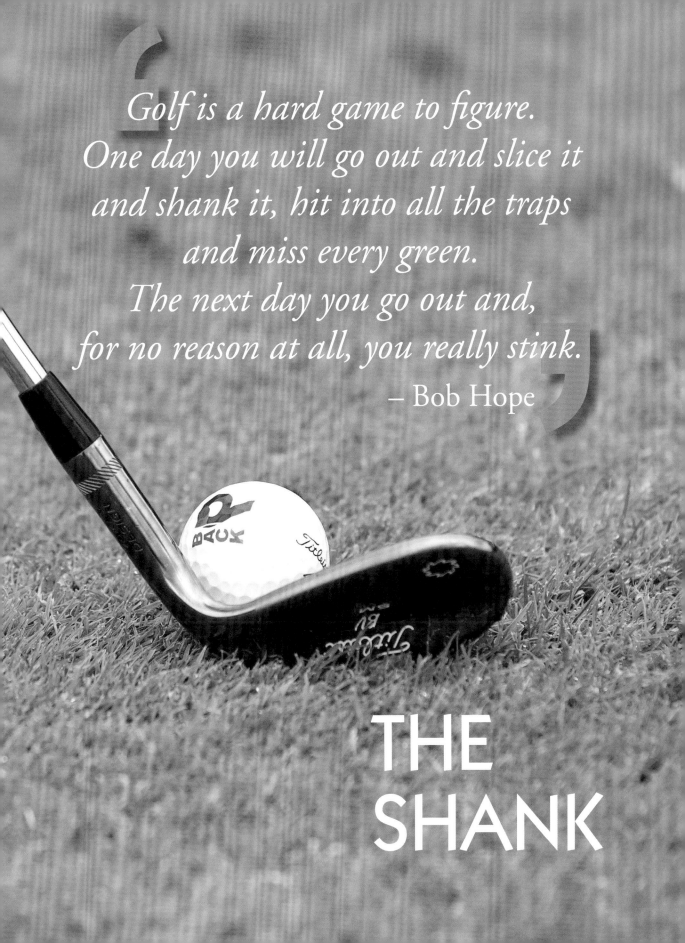

Golf is a hard game to figure.
One day you will go out and slice it
and shank it, hit into all the traps
and miss every green.
The next day you go out and,
for no reason at all, you really stink.
— Bob Hope

THE
SHANK

The Shank (a.k.a. The Irish Hook)

This is most destructive of all bad shots. I'm frequently asked for a 'cure' for this terrible affliction, which at some time or another has affected pretty much all of us.

Funny isn't it. We shank one ball on the course then on returning to the clubhouse offer embarrassed excuses, yet we forget to mention the snap hook or wild slices that we executed with equal panache. This is because not only can a shank destroy an entire round, it knocks our confidence, peace of mind and tranquillity. Stating the obvious, my advice is always the same, work out why you're doing it then eliminate it with practice.

These awful shots tend to happen when we have a wedge in our hands, because the very nature of the shot encourages a shorter backswing with less time to manipulate the downswing.

They're the result of hitting the ball off the socket of the club and can be attributed to one of three different causes, in the images opposite Simon has managed to demonstrate all three:

- the most frequent, rolling the wrists on the backswing

- standing too near the ball at address causing poor posture

- at address having too much weight on the heels, causing the weight to move onto the toes at impact.

The underlying reason for all of the above is usually a poor posture.

Simon

On my return to playing I was afflicted with the most horrendous shanks from 100 yards in. The experience is one I'll never forget and the feeling I would get when faced with a relatively simple wedge shot is difficult to explain but I can only describe it as blind panic. I'm still occasionally struck by it now. It was caused not only by rustiness, but everything Peter has just described. His work with me has built my confidence and his practice routines have been a real benefit.

Now we've established the cause of this terrible affliction, how do we fix it?

It's simple really, PRACTICE!

Try this simple practice routine. All you need is a an alignment stick, a wedge, some practice balls and a small practice area. It really helps eliminate shanks and is also an excellent exercise to help you keep your hands connected and ahead of the clubhead for *all* your short shots.

Take a wedge and extend the shaft with an alignment stick. Grip the club with the extension resting against the front side. It will feel a bit strange but just swing back and through making sure that the shaft extension doesn't leave your side. This ensures that your hands stay ahead of the clubhead, your body turns correctly and stops flicking the club at impact with your hands.

DO NOT FORGET — **Your head and chest follow as you swing through.**

OTHER PRACTICE DRILLS

The grip extension

Here's another great drill to try using an alignment stick.

All rubber grips have a small hole in the top of the grip. Enlarge the hole a little, no damage will be done to the club in doing so, get an alignment stick and slide it into the grip and down into the shaft until the club is a similar length to a driver.

Lodge the end into your tummy, gripping the club normally move the triangle created by your shoulders and arms back and forth by turning your shoulders. This gives you the feel of turning back and through as a unit, including your head, on the follow-through.

Throwing a ball

Earlier in the book, I explained the similarities between throwing a ball and the golf swing. It's particularly relevant to chipping. A good chipping action is as simple and natural as throwing a ball and yet many who can throw a ball struggle to chip. The reason is that when chipping, there's a tendency to swing with our hands, whilst when throwing a ball we do so with our arms and shoulders.

Here's an excellent practice drill to help you improve your touch and feel around the green. Next time you're practicing start off by throwing a few balls at the target, then throw some with your eyes closed. Feel how your arms control your throw. Then start chipping and try to create the same feel.

Chipping one-handed

A really helpful practice exercise is to chip one-handed.

Grip the club with your bottom hand and chip the ball at the target. Feel how your arm and shoulders control your swing and ensure that your swing moves on the right plane. Repeat it with your eyes closed and concentrate on how your arm and shoulders feel during the swing and then try and feel where the ball has gone.

Then add your front hand and try to repeat the feel of chipping one-handed.

Chipping with feet together

This is a brilliant drill to help reduce your leg movement whilst chipping.

Address the ball with your feet together then swing normally. The stance prevents you from moving your legs and instead you will feel your arms and shoulders controlling the swing.

This exercise is strongly recommended for those who have too much leg movement when chipping.

Chipping yips

Yips are horrific and can ruin any round and all the enjoyment from playing. Hard work and experimentation are really the only cures.

Think outside the box. If you work hard you can defeat most things, just keep an open mind, even the daftest ideas can sometimes help you turn the corner.

Anyone with the dreaded chipping yips should give the cack-handed grip a try straight away.

It's an extension of the reverse putting grip where the top hand stays close to the body on the backswing and the bottom hand dominates through impact keeping the follow-through wide.

It tends to work up to about 30 yards but do practice it first.

Drill for eliminating excess leg movement

This exercise can be used for shots up 30/40 yards. Take your normal stance then move your back foot twelve inches behind your front foot. Your weight is now automatically advanced onto your front leg. Swing back with your hands and arms, keeping your top arm straight, notice how much easier it is to take the club back with your hands and arms.

Swing down and through keeping your lower arm straight and your head and chest following through towards the target.

It isn't just a practice drill, it also can work for you on the course although it's wise to practice it beforehand.

and finally...

One final thought for when you're practicing these little chip shots around the green. Have you ever tried practicing with your eyes closed?

Give it a go, set up normally for the shot, close your eyes and hit the ball, the feedback when you open your eyes will be interesting. You'll need a few shots to get used to the idea, but it will definitely provide you with more understanding of the imagination and feel of the shot and it's fun!

Logic will get you from A to B, imagination will take you everywhere.
– Albert Einstein

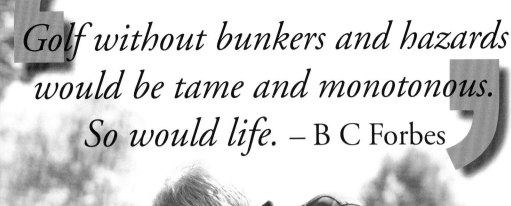

Golf without bunkers and hazards would be tame and monotonous. So would life. – B C Forbes

Bunkers

Setup

- shuffle your feet for a solid base
- position ball just inside your front heel
- weight mainly on your front foot.

40% 60%

- feet, hips and shoulders aligned fractionally open
- clubface square to target.

The splash shot

The perfect bunker shot is a rhythmic explosion. It's all about setup and follow-through. Whatever your technique, if you setup correctly and attack the sand with your follow-through the ball will come out. Most failures are caused by quitting on the shot.

The weight on your front foot creates a slightly steeper downswing enabling you to take the sand first and then the ball leaving the club to do the work. Never try to lift the ball out of the bunker by flicking the hands at impact.

When deciding how hard to hit a bunker shot, Jack Nicklaus advises imagining that the shot you're playing is twice as far as it would be if chipping from grass. My advice is that the best way of deciding how hard to hit these shots and how much sand to take is:

PRACTICE!

Backswing

- maintain your weight on your front foot with your knees flexed throughout your backswing this enables your wrists to break earlier and a slightly steeper backswing
- the open alignment creates an out to in swing, enabling the club to slide under the ball on the follow-through.

40% - 60%

Follow-through

- length of your follow-through matches your backswing
- swing smoothly, letting the club do the work
- keep both feet firmly placed in the sand throughout
- follow flight of ball with your head and shoulders after impact.

30% - 70%

Plugged ball in bunker

We've all experienced the poached egg. Usually it happens at the worst possible time. You walk up to the bunker and there it is, your worst nightmare surrounded by a circular ridge of sand. All previous advice has to be discarded and a totally new approach is needed if you're to get the ball out of the bunker and rescue your round.

30% 70%

For the best results:

- shuffle your feet a little to create a solid base

- place more weight on your front foot, for a steeper downswing

- ball further back in your stance – approximately in the middle

- square the clubface up, or even slightly close it, to eliminate the bounce of the sole

- square up your feet, shoulders and hips to the target

- go digging for Australia at impact by continuing the downward movement and striking the sand hard one or two inches behind the ball keeping the clubface square throughout (If you're in Australia, dig for England!)

- never try lifting the ball, it's an explosion!

- allow for the fact that the ball will come out without any backspin so will roll further than usual.

Downhill lies

30%

70%

The key to the downhill bunker shot is your stance.

Your hips and shoulders must be parallel to the sand with your weight remaining on your lower foot at all times. Your shoulders and hips go with the slope so the club follows the slope.

30%

70%

30%

70%

70%
30%

Uphill lies

With the uphill shot, again the key is your stance.

Your hips and shoulders must be parallel to the sand with your weight remaining on your lower foot at all times so the club follows the slope. WARNING! Avoid the temptation to put your weight on your front foot!

30%
70%

30%
70%

Bunker strategy

Think smart. Don't try playing that one in a thousand shot. We've all tried it and know it doesn't work.

Before entering the bunker, look closely at the quality of the sand and the lie of the ball as they have a big influence on how you should play the shot.

The amount of sand you take when playing from a bunker varies considerably according to the speed of the swing and the quality of the sand. The faster you swing and the lighter and drier the sand, the more sand you can take whereas those of us with slower, more rhythmic swings or when playing out of heavy sand need take less.

Next, assess the target and terrain. If you can't go directly for the pin, think laterally. Your main aim should always be to take your medicine and get the ball out.

'The Sands of Nakajima'
Tommy Nakajima battles with the Road Hole bunker and comes out a very distant second.

Remember poor Tsuneyuki (Tommy) Nakajima, on the 17th – 'the Road Hole', in the third round of the 1978 Open at St Andrews? He was in contention until he putted his third shot into the Road Hole bunker and then proceeded to take four attempts to extricate himself by trying to be too clever. Tommy was no slouch on the golf course and in his career won 48 tournaments on the Japanese circuit and was even ranked in the world top 10 players for 85 weeks. The media would subsequently refer to the incident as *The sands of Nakajima*.

It happens to the best of players, don't let it happen to you!

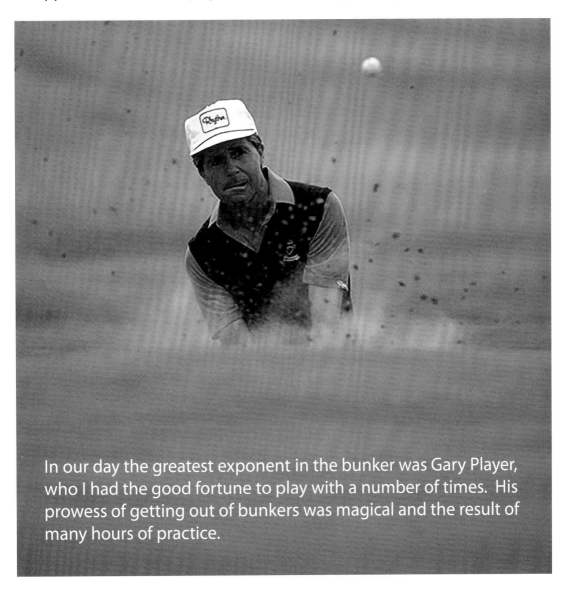

In our day the greatest exponent in the bunker was Gary Player, who I had the good fortune to play with a number of times. His prowess of getting out of bunkers was magical and the result of many hours of practice.

Wet sand

Unless there's a lip to go over, play these shots as you would a pitch so take either your gap wedge or 48° pitching wedge to eliminate the bounce.

Narrow your stance with 60% of your weight on your front foot, grip about two inches further down the shaft than usual and with the clubface square to the target aim to clip the ball off the surface just below its equator.

Let the loft of the club do its work, at impact it's very easy to forget and then try and scoop the ball up with the bottom hand. Don't become short and jerky, remain relaxed. Keep your lower body still throughout the swing.

If you need more height on the shot, take the more lofted sand wedge, repeat the same technique, remembering to let the loft of the club do the work.

30 to 100 yds

This is acknowledged as one of the most difficult shots in golf.

Too much sand and the ball embarrassingly falls 60 yards short or not enough and the ball can career some 30 yards over the green. Half an inch between a great and a bad shot!

Thinking back to my tournament days, when my ball found its way into a bunker some 80 to 100 yards short of the putting surface, I was always relieved when my ball was lying well because it left me a much easier shot.

I would enter the bunker with a 9 iron or pitching wedge in hand, with every intention of making the required full and graceful swing.

Having taken my stance, one final look at the intended target would reveal the stands directly behind the green full of knowledgeable spectators. There were then 5 possibilities, although through your own experience you may know of more.

Scenario 1 – I swing too fast, losing my equilibrium and striking the sand 2 to 3 inches behind the ball, which just about clambers out of the bunker. Even hundred yards from the green, the mutterings of, *"even I could do better than that",* are clearly audible from the stands!

Scenario 2 – I take less, but still too much sand, and the shot still comes up way short. The mumblings from the spectators are slightly less critical and a lot more understanding.

Scenario 3 – instead of striking the ball just below its middle, I strike it just above, the shot is thinned straight into the face of the bunker and worse, the ball is plugged in the face. I have to take an unplayable penalty and drop the ball back into the bunker, facing the same shot all over again!

A yawn is a silent shout.
– Gilbert K Chesterton

Scenario 4 – I strike the ball smack bang on its equator, it skims the bunker face traveling like an Exocet missile heading for a lady just pouring herself a cup of tea from her flask in row G. Much panic and shouts of *'fore'* are coming from the caddy and me as we imagine the impending and grovelling apology to the spectators, or even worse, a lawsuit.

Everybody now ducks and dives out of the way, the ball ricochets around the stand like a pinball, the flask and its contents shower the spectators in range and eventually things settle down amid much laughter from the spectators not in the immediate danger zone.

> *I know I'm getting better at golf because I am hitting fewer spectators.*
> – Gerald Ford

Scenario 5 – The best of all – I hit it absolutely spot on, swinging the club slow and methodically, clipping the ball off the surface and watch as it lands on the centre of the green coming to an abrupt stop on the second bounce, raising my hand to acknowledge the applause.

> *Applause waits on success.*
> – Benjamin Franklin

I hope these pages will help you avoid scenarios 1 to 4.

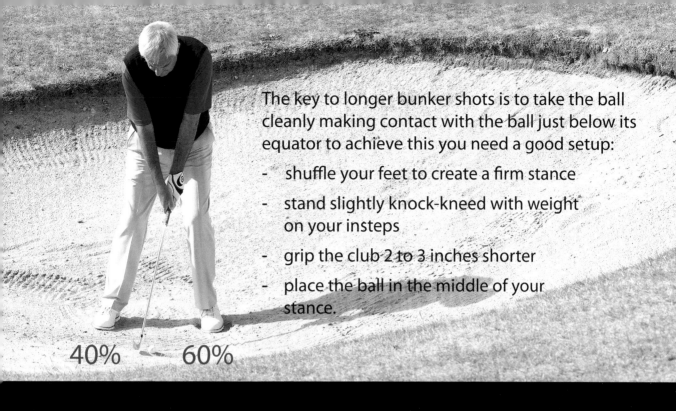

The key to longer bunker shots is to take the ball cleanly making contact with the ball just below its equator to achieve this you need a good setup:

- shuffle your feet to create a firm stance

- stand slightly knock-kneed with weight on your insteps

- grip the club 2 to 3 inches shorter

- place the ball in the middle of your stance.

40%   60%

Never attack the sand on these shots, sweep the ball away letting the loft of the club do its work.

Swing slowly and gracefully, imagining your swing is a pendulum with the same length back and through. A fast or jerky swing causes lack of balance.

40%   60%   30%   70%

Choosing the right club

If your ball is well positioned in a bunker 80 yards from the green, the most important decision is which club to use. This is obviously influenced by a combination of factors:

- the lie and distance of the shot

- the weather and condition of the course – wind and rain and the course conditions have a big influence

- what lies between you and the green

- height of the bunker lip – the club must have enough loft to give the ball the height to carry over the lip. I have a good tip for this. Take a tee peg and place it on the face of the club and then compare to the angle of ascent needed to escape the bunker as in the images below.

Always remember your main priority is to get the ball out!

100 yds+

- don't take on too much

- choose the right club

- take a firm stance

- grip an inch down the shaft

- keep the legs and hips passive, it's the top half of our body that dominates

- sweep the ball off the surface

- make contact with the ball just under its equator

- at address hover the club an inch off the sand.

Good practice tip:

If your golf club has a practice bunker, practicing a full shot with a 5 or 6 iron can be very rewarding. It improves your ball striking and certainly shows up your faults. It wasn't uncommon to catch Seve or Greg Norman practicing on the beach next to the links.

A good player who is a great putter is a match for any golfer. A great hitter who cannot putt is a match for no one.
– Ben Sayers

PUTTING
The business end of things

A 'gimme' can be best defined as an agreement between two golfers, neither of whom can putt very well.
— Unknown

So many books have been written on putting – good ones too! How many ways have you heard it described? *'It's a game within a game'*, *'it's a game apart'*, *'it's the most important part of the game', 'drive for show, putt for dough!'*

All true, you never see the tournament winner putting badly.

The putt is the final shot of the hole just played, if you've holed a great putt, you take that momentum onto the next but if you've three-putted or missed a short one, your disappointment and frustration can lead to over-compensation and more mistakes.

I think it's great to see people my age having a putting lesson. It shows they understand the importance of this part of their game. When putting you can be a match for anyone. You don't need power to putt!

I remember during my playing days receiving a letter from my bank demanding that I pay off a loan. A week later I was standing over a six-foot putt to win a tournament and the cash I needed. I didn't care how I did it, I just needed that damn ball to drop in the hole. To onlookers I was in deep concentration, in reality, I was actually praying that my years of practice would pay off – that's pressure. As it turned out, the practice paid off and my bank manager was a very happy man.

People get bogged down in too much theory. When the words *'must do this or that'*, enter the conversation I withdraw a little. To be a good putter you need technique, experience, feeling, imagination and a lot of hard work.

Putting is truly individual for us all. What works for one often doesn't work for another. Over the years we've all developed our own unique routines and techniques, (whether text book or not). I would never say to someone, *'you must!'* but there are a few basic principles which are followed by all the very best putters.

This section provides you with a guide to these principles that when combined with plenty of practice, will make a difference.

The grip

How you grip your putter is down to individual choice, whether the result of years of playing or simply something that is currently working well for you. Your putting grip is, however, key to your putting consistency.

There are many different ways to grip the putter, the four main ones are below. Then there are other variations, such as the thickness of the grip and the different shaft lengths. The permutations are humongous.

Pros can wax lyrical about certain grips, putter lengths or grip thicknesses but in the end it all comes down to what feels and works best for you. We all tinker and experiment but the very best putters tend to stick to the same old rusty putter and the same putting style year after year.

Whatever the combination, you should always ensure that your hands and forearms work together.

How tightly should you hold the putter? This is very important. A tight putting grip causes tension, reduces feel and leads to missed short putts. Grip the club as if it is a wand or a paintbrush, with authority but not so tightly that you strangle the feeling out of your hands.

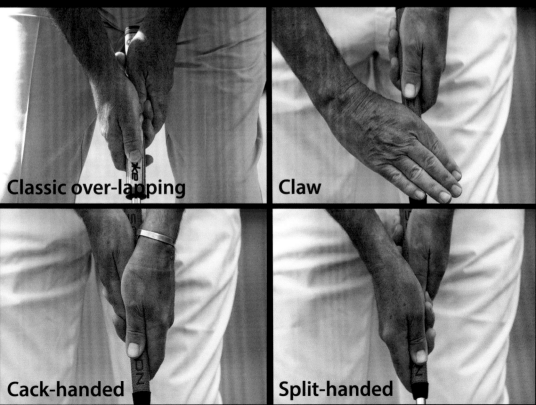

Classic over-lapping

Claw

Cack-handed

Split-handed

The stance

For most of us, the putter is the shortest club in the bag and, as with all golf shots, good posture is essential to provide the solid platform you need to putt consistently well.

When putting you bend primarily from the waist and it's your spine and shoulders that create the pendulum movement without moving the rest of the body.

At address, your eyes should be over the ball or as close as possible with the ball fractionally forward of centre to ensure a slightly upward strike.

Lining up your putt

Many putts are missed through poor alignment. This is an increasing problem for us as we get older. Here are some ideas for you to try:

- line up the putter head first, only taking up your stance when you're happy the putter is lined up correctly

- as we age, one eye can become weaker than the other, which might affect our ability to line up the clubhead. If this is your experience, experiment by closing one eye, then the other, when lining up so you can work out which eye works best for you

- check that your shoulders are square to the line

- choose a spot on your chosen line and aim for it.

The stroke

Note how, in the image, the legs, head and hips remain still throughout the stroke, only the shoulders and arms move creating a pendulum movement.

For short putts, the angle created by your stance, (bending from the waist), will cause the shoulders to tilt rather than turn. It's only when you have a longer putt that your shoulders need to turn a fraction causing the putter to go back slightly inside the line.

Here are some sound principles to help:

- position the ball slightly forward of centre at address – this produces an arc, (see the red dotted line where the putter head is lower on the backswing and is travelling on an upward motion when it hits the ball). This produces topspin, which helps the ball roll more smoothly making it easier to control. If the ball is behind centre at address, the putter will strike the ball in a downward motion causing the ball to bounce with a loss of control and accuracy

- the hands and forearms must work as one unit

- don't decelerate the stroke through impact – as with all your shots, you must accelerate through impact keeping the clubhead moving along the line. Many missed putts are due to deceleration at impact, often caused by uncertainty. If you're going to miss a putt, at least miss it with conviction

- the head must remain still throughout – resist the temptation to have a peek on those awful 3 footers to see if the ball goes in the hole. Try practicing this length with your eyes closed. The feeling and success rate is incredibly high.

Important fact

As part of my research for the book I contacted NASA who have confirmed that no putt that has finished short of the hole has ever gone in.

Nothing matters more in putting than it should be kept simple and positive.

— Laura Davies

Feel and imagination

> *Imagination is more important than knowledge.*
> — Albert Einstein

Feel and imagination come with practice. When we're young, hitting 100's of balls isn't a problem but a few years on it's a little different. We have no excuse for not practicing our putting – that is until the back muscles tell us otherwise! Hard work can't guarantee perfection but it does give us the confidence and belief that after all that work we really do deserve to putt well.

How far should the putter head travel? I've played with some great players that stroke the ball beautifully and I've played with a few that curtail the follow-through with more of a punch. I wouldn't advise you to do one or the other and refer you to Harry Vardon's sage advice:

> *As regards stance and manner of hitting the ball, it is for the individual to discover on the green the means that suit him best with the club that gives him most confidence.*
> — Harry Vardon

With more practice comes greater understanding, you don't get what you wish for you get what you work for!

Reading the greens

There is no similarity between golf and putting, they are two different games. One played through the air, and the other on the ground.
— Ben Hogan

We all know that putting isn't just about technique or feel, it's about understanding how outside agencies can affect the ball, how slopes influence it, the dampness, texture, even the colour of the grass. It's been said that truly great putters are born but with practice and experience we can all achieve the higher standards we crave.

Our work on the putting surface starts some 30 metres short of the green!

When approaching the green you need to be looking at the lie of the land and where the slopes are that will influence the roll of the ball. A tree close to the edge of a green could be sucking the moisture out of the soil, making that area dry, hard and fast. On a sloping green, the water will drain to the lowest area making it softer, greener and possibly slower to putt on. Perhaps the sand from an adjacent bunker has found its way onto the green, making the surface firmer and faster. Once you're standing on the putting surface you may see certain slopes and be influenced by a bank to the side of the green.

Putting is a fascinating aggravating, wonderful, terrible and most incomprehensible part of the game of golf.
— Arnold Palmer

Have you ever tried putting across a ten-metre slope? The slope will have little effect for the first few metres because of the speed of the ball but as it loses momentum the slope kicks in. So instead of chatting with your playing partners as you approach the green, be alert.

Many of the top players look into the hole and study the area around the hole before they putt because it's around the hole that the ball is moving at its slowest and so the condition of the green surrounding the hole has the greatest influence over their putt.

Always remember to take into account the weather conditions, wind can influence the line of a putt as can moisture.

And finally...

I'm constantly reminded of Mrs Ben Hogan's advice to her husband in response to his persistent complaints about missing too many 20 foot putts. She very simply and logically told him to hit his approach shots closer to the hole!

It's a marriage. If I had to choose between my wife and my putter, well, I'd miss her.
– Gary Player

Putting practice drills

Every player has their own favourite putting drill, usually repetition-based, here are some good ones:

Clock putting – this is where you place balls all around the hole at lengths ranging from 3 to 10 feet. It's a favourite of Phil Mickelson.

20 putts routine – this requires you to hole 20 straight two or three foot putts in a row, and if you miss one you have to start all over again. Believe me the pressure builds as you approach the magic 20 mark.

Coin drill (see images below) – this is a great way of practicing keeping the putter head low through the stroke and hitting the ball on the up. Place the ball on a coin such as a 50p and ensure that you hit each putt without moving or even touching the coin on the follow-through. Keep your head still and focused on the coin throughout.

Two alignment stick drills

The first one, is to address the ball gripping both the putter and the alignment stick with the stick pressed into your stomach. Then swing the putter back and through using just your arms and shoulders. This promotes a pendulum movement.

The one below encourages the body to remain still during the putting stroke. Push an alignment stick into the green next to you, take your stance against it, then putt as normal taking care to keep the front of your body static against the stick.

1977

Golf is played mainly on a five-and-a-half-inch course... the space between your ears.
— Bobby Jones

Missing a short putt does not mean you have to hit your next drive out of bounds.
— Henry Cotton

Golf is 80% mental, 10% ability and 10% luck.
— Jack Nicklaus

Placing the ball in the right position for your next shot is 80% of winning golf.
— Ben Hogan

The time leading up to my Ryder Cup appearance was both hectic and memorable. Most of the memories are good but one always leaps out to remind me how the game builds you up only to knock you straight back down again.

The week before, most of us played in the Tour Players Championship at Foxhills, in Surrey. I'd been on good form in the lead-up and charged through the field. I even broke the course record in the third round shooting 65!

Posing with the card after my course record 65.

The following day, the final round couldn't have been more different as I disintegrated to a shocking 79. *The Irish Times* quite fairly pegged me as '*hapless*'. In truth, I was nervous and my swing on the day felt out of sync. This, combined with poor course management, led to me throwing away a tournament when a clear head would've seen me through to a comfortable victory.

Amazingly, despite playing poorly, I was still just about holding it together and arrived at the 18th one shot ahead of Neil Coles. Meanwhile, Neil who had started 10 shots behind me, was relaxing in the clubhouse on the assumption he was going to finish second.

I'd birdied the 18th the previous day and my only thought was, '*Come on you old bugger, same again and we're home and dry*'. The adrenalin was pumping. There I was about to make my Ryder Cup debut, one shot clear in a tournament that guaranteed my place in the prestigious end-of-season World Match-Play at Wentworth. One dreadful drive later and I was fighting to finish second. I'd blown it. I'd got ahead of myself and the golf that had elevated me on the previous day brought me back down to earth with a resounding thwump!

Play smart

Canny golfers plot their way round the course making the most of their physical resources, choosing the easiest position for their next shot whether it's an approach from a better angle or an easier putt.

I remember playing with Lee Trevino one year in the Australian Open. He gave me a master class in strategy. It was a superb course running fast with incredibly quick greens. I remember he would deliberately land the ball short of the hole, leaving himself simple uphill putts and the best opportunity to score well – which he did. Meanwhile I was trying hard to impress, too hard! I was enthusiastically attacking everything leaving my approaches in the most difficult positions and three putting far too often as a result. Lee sailed through the cut and I just scraped through.

We're all capable of moments of madness. After a competition, *'if only'* are probably the most commonly heard words in the bar afterwards. How many times have you sat in the clubhouse listening to one of your group mumbling, *'If only I hadn't…'?*

If a par on the 18th guarantees a win, it's not the best time to try a once in a lifetime shot – eliminate as many risks as you can, play within your limitations and plot your way to victory.

On par fives and those long fours which can no longer be reached in two, don't try to achieve the impossible, that often leads to disaster. Instead, keep a cool head and play within yourself. Think position over power.

How often have we seen the top players lay up seemingly way too short? They all have their favourite shots and yardages, they use to their best advantage whenever possible.

Another sound piece of advice is, be alert on the course. Watch your opponents' shots for hints of what might happen to yours. See how they play the hole and learn. Keep your eyes open checking out the holes ahead where possible for useful information such as the flag positions.

The magnificent seven

Trust – always trust your own game, good golf is impossible until you can.

Patience – is key to all good rounds so try not to rush things.

Mental rhythm – we all have a natural rhythm at which we play our best. You know when you feel comfortable, stick to it.

Stay in the now – too many players get ahead of themselves don't be one of them.

Know your limits – always play within yourself especially under pressure.

Picture the shot – try to visualise each shot in your mind before you play, it works!

Be decisive – bad shots are caused by indecision. Commit yourself.

Bournemouth Sumrie Fourball

I had the great fortune of partnering Tony Jacklin in the Sumrie Four Ball Championship at Queens Park in Bournemouth. Obviously playing with Tony, US Open champion in 1970 and Open champion in 1969 was fantastic!

Jimmy Tarbuck, the great comedian and also a very good golfer was appearing in Bournemouth at the time and joined us for one of the practice rounds along with Clive Clark, former Walker Cup and Ryder Cup player. Needless to say when word got out Jimmy Tarbuck and Tony Jacklin were in town the crowds flocked to Queens Park.

There were no barriers keeping the crowd back from the players on the course except for a small picket fence keeping them off the tees. On one tee whilst going through my pre-shot routine I heard a lot of sniggering and muted laughter behind me. Stopping to see what I was missing, it turned out I was the cause of it!

The winter before I had represented England with Nick Faldo in the World Cup in Manila, it was during that visit I had bought a large garish leather belt which was decorated with a number of symbols that looked like signs of the Zodiac but on closer inspection were Kama Sutra positions. In my defence I was a young man of the 70's! That morning I dressed in a pair of flared trousers (all the rage at the time) that required a wide belt, I had put it on without a second thought.

It was mid-day on the South coast and the temperature rose so I took off my sweater revealing the belt I had completely forgotten I was wearing. Jimmy was intrigued and looking more closely quickly realised what the symbols represented. He duly brought the figures to the attention of everyone nearby, asking their thoughts with great charm and hilarity!

Looking back I don't know what possessed me to buy that belt in the first place and worse still, wear it in public but then that was the 70's!

Today I cringe at the memory!

Practice drills

Practice puts brains into muscles.
Sam Snead

*They say practice makes perfect, of course
it doesn't. For the vast majority of golfers
practice merely consolidates imperfection.*
– Henry Longhurst

Practice

What pleasure there is to be had when taking a tube of balls onto the practice ground hitting them whilst trying to improve our technique, pausing occasionally to survey the world around us. Despite hitting thousands upon thousands of golf balls in my 40 year career, I still get that incredible buzz when I hit that one perfect shot.

Alas with age the ball doesn't stay in the air for long these days!

Saying that, Henry Longhurst is right, there's little point practicing imperfection. Unless you're merely warming up, to make practice worthwhile always try to have some idea what you 're working on from a technical point of view.

A good way is to start by hitting 20 balls with your feet together just to get a rhythm and balance before moving onto a longer club. I suggest starting with a 7 iron.

Another great exercise is explained on page 144. Take your 9 iron or wedge address the ball normally then withdraw your back foot some 12 inches. Your weight will now be prominently on your front foot with your back foot acting as a support. You'll now feel how through the hitting area your chest and head follow the flight of the ball with your front leg acting in a pivotal function. This works wonderfully for those shots of 30 to 40 yards.

I strongly suggest you practice your short game far more than your long game. It's less tiring and helps produce more feel and greater imagination on the golf course. Once again, use the golf balls you generally play, not range balls.

Practice does not make perfect.
Only perfect practice makes perfect.
— Vince Lombardi

I got rhythm...

The old pros would tell us to slowly count to three on the backswing, saying four at impact. If you feel your swing is too fast you could for a few pounds purchase a metronome, then setting it to a slow rhythmical setting marry your swing to that beat. Better still, you can now download a metronome app on to your mobile phone and take it out with you when you practice. The first few shots are sure to destroy your timing but if you persevere it will help you gain a better rhythm. The aim is then to carry that new found rhythm onto the course.

What a load of balls!

Nigeria in the early 1970's, was the first stop of the African Tour, which at that time was the season curtain-raiser. After Nigeria, we would travel to Zambia, Botswana, Kenya and the Ivory Coast.

Travelling to Lagos in those days was interesting to say the least, the plane would be virtually full of budding young players in search of fame and cash. Each of us with tournament golf bags, enough clothing and luggage to see us through a two week stint, PLUS a practice ball bag full of some 100 plus balls. Thankfully excess baggage didn't exist at the time.

There were no practice ranges in those days, at the end of each day's play we would go out onto the first fairway, send our caddies the appropriate distance and then fire the balls at them. At the end of each session we hoped they returned with the same number, or more, than we started with. There were often up to 20 caddies all doing the same thing, how we never killed anyone remains a mystery to me!

In return, when the final tournament finished we would give the caddies the remaining balls which they would then sell to the local golfers.

Going through baggage control in the airports was always interesting. Often the officers would question why we had these strange looking sticks whilst the practice ball bag was often referred to as *'What are these? Bombs?'*

I always thought it was amusing when being questioned about these mysterious looking *'bombs'* the officers would regularly bounce them on the ground to see what might happen.

New visitors to Lagos and the interior were tipped off by the more experienced players to place a few dollars in our passports. Sound advice, those few dollars often got us through road blocks a bit quicker.

All hail the men with a van!

In the early days struggling on the tour, players often shared motorised caravans, converted vans or similar, doing whatever necessary to keep costs down.

My first Swiss Open was played at the swish resort Crans Montana. Four of us shared a Morris 1100. We tied our pencil bags onto the roof rack and squeezed our luggage and my size 13 shoes into any crevice we could find or create.

We also all shared one bedroom, (I think the management said it was a room for three). It rained heavily so four sets of waterproofs and sodden golf shoes didn't half make the room smell!

Two of the players would drive to the continental events in an old Post Office van which they also slept in. Story has it that following the Swiss Open they drove through the night to get to the next tournament in Germany, parking up in the early hours in a perfectly prepared field close to the clubhouse. They were woken the following morning by the worst hailstorm in history or so they thought. In fact, the hailstones were golf balls, in the dead of the night they had camped right in the middle of the practice ground!

If you call on God to improve the results of a shot while it is still in motion, you are using "an outside agency" and subject to appropriate penalties under the rules of golf.

– Henry Longhurst

A quick reminder of the practice drills in the book

Head position drill
How to ensure your head position is tall and proud at address (page 32)

The Peter Thomson setup
How to create the perfect stance, posture and alignment from the late five-time Open champion (page 32)

Throwing the ball & swinging one-handed
Helps you with your long and short games
(pages 55 & 140)

Hitting the wall
For practicing posture and impact positions. Can be done anywhere, all you need is a wall! (Page 57)

Feet together
Helps with your width of stance and improve your chipping (Pages 70 &142)

Circle of power
Helps you increase your power especially off the tee (Page 75)

Rolling rolling rolling
Helps you practice the top spin drive. All you need is a tennis racket (Page 76)

Wrist break
Helps you break your wrists early and effectively to produce more power (Page 90)

Curing the shank – Chipping with alignment stick
Help ensure your arms and wrists are in the correct position at impact (Page 138)

Grip extension
A drill to encourage the shoulders to turn correctly whilst chipping (Page 139)

Curing chipping yips
For those with chipping woes (Page 143)

Chipping with back foot behind
Helps improve your chipping (Page 144)

Putting drills
Drills to encourage the correct movement whilst putting (Page 174 & 175)

Acknowledgements

There are so many people to thank for helping me with this project.

My thanks go to:

Jezz Ellwood – for his expert advice and insight

Peter Dazeley – for allowing to use his photographs of my days on tour

Jez Tomlinson – for his wonderful hospitality and generosity

Paul O'Hagen & Tony Donnaruma at Titleist & Footjoy

David Hewlett – for giving me confidence from the outset that this was a good project

Those who were kind enough to proof-read our various drafts:

Nigel Blenkarne – Master Professional and director of golf

Paul Brown – General Manager Hockley GC, Winchester

Gary Smith – PGA advanced fellow professional and EGU elite squad coach

Keith Mannering – his friendship and tireless work for worthy causes

Tim Seabrook – friend and champion fund-raiser for many charities especially Cystic Fibrosis

Geoff and Gayna Healy – true self-admitted pedants!

Richard Lock – for all his IT and website expertise, enthusiasm and support